Praise for *BREAKFAST FOR AL*
AND REVELATIOI

"DuFord has created a series of m_   _...orous travel stories in which no local foods, material realities, or local rituals are off-
limits. *Breakfast for Alligators* is a joy to read."

Gregory Hubbs, editor of *Transitions Abroad*

"Intrepid and chronically curious, Darrin DuFord charges into the more
obscure corners of Latin America and brings back revealing, sometimes
bizarre details. Warning: may inspire impulse plane-ticket purchases."

Zora O'Neill, author of *All Strangers Are Kin:*
Adventures in Arabic and the Arab World

"DuFord captures the best of travel writing—by turn informative and
entertaining, often hilarious, sometimes moving... He takes us on one
wild ride after another."

Tony Perrottet, author of *Napoleon's Privates:*
2,500 Years of History Unzipped

"In a world full of overwrought and contrived travel stories, Darrin
DuFord's collection, *Breakfast for Alligators*, is a breath of fresh air: open,
honest, and in love with the world (and its many flavors) in a way that
makes you yearn to go along with DuFord as he follows his curiosity to
the far corners of the Americas."

Frank Bures, author of *The Geography of Madness: Penis*
Thieves, Voodoo Death, and the Search for the Meaning of
the World's Strangest Syndromes

"Darrin DuFord's thoughtful, reflective prose offers a short episodic-
type glimpse of the moments in question—competing wine festivals that
weren't all that competitive in Chile, a slice of the drumming life in Montevideo, Uruguay....There's plenty to entertain."

Chris Backe, *One Weird Globe*

"Darrin DuFord's latest magnum opus vividly takes us from the steamy
New Orleans suburbs to the jungles of Guyana to the coffee-covered hills
of Nicaragua and beyond. This is more than breakfast: it's a readable,
enjoyable feast, best consumed any time of day or night."

David Farley, author of *An Irreverent Curiosity*

Also by Darrin DuFord

Is There a Hole in the Boat? Tales of Travel in Panama Without a Car

Breakfast
for
Alligators

Quests,
Showdowns,
and Revelations
in the Americas

Darrin DuFord

TILTED
HAT
PRESS

For Memere and Pepere

"Journey by Bottle" first appeared in *Gastronomica*

"The Search for the Golden Fleece" first appeared in the *San Francisco Chronicle*

"A Dialog of Echoes," "The Peanut Fiends of Guayaquil," "Coup in A Coup: a Tale of Venezuelan Tipple," "Subdued by Street Vendors," and "Showdown at the West Esplanade Canal" first appeared in *Perceptive Travel* in slightly different forms

"Barbecue-flavored Mealworms" first appeared in *McSweeney's Internet Tendency* (McSweeneys.net)

"A Planet within a Planet" first appeared in *Narratively* under the title "Off the Deep End in Captain Karl's Homemade Yellow Submarine"

"What the Walls Taught Me" first appeared in *The Smart Set*

"Chowhounding Peru, from Anticuchos to Zaino" and "Beyond a Shadow of a Snout: a Saturday in Otavalo" first appeared in *GoNomad* in slightly different forms

"The Comb of Rebellion" first appeared in *The Panama Report* in a slightly different form

"Journey by Bottle" won a gold medal in the 2013 Solas Awards

"Showdown at the West Esplanade Canal" won a silver medal in the 2010 Solas Awards

"Subdued by Street Vendors" won a silver medal in the 2009 Solas Awards

"A Planet within a Planet" won a bronze medal in the 2015 North American Travel Journalist's Association Awards and a bronze medal in the 2016 Solas Awards

"The Comb of Rebellion" won a bronze medal in the 2008 Solas Awards

Table of Contents

Breakfast for Alligators

Introduction: What Is Distance?

A lot of shrinking seems to be afflicting travel lately. Much attention has been focused on the hands of globalization pinching remote patches of the planet, squeezing the earth into what may seem like a ball of assimilation, leaving us a landscape with less isolation and diversity. Thus, travel delivers a cheapened experience for both the visitor and the visited, making the world smaller.

Or does it? I have begun to ask if the opposite may be true. A recent reverb-soaked moment in Montevideo, Uruguay, forced my hand. As I stood facing the city's central commercial thoroughfare, 18 de Julio Avenue, "I Want to Know What Love Is" by the group Foreigner sprang from a magazine kiosk. At first, I was tempted to claim that yes, this is even more evidence that the planet is hemorrhaging diversity. I was in a country of mostly white people, mostly wearing t-shirts, who enjoy the same music I had listened to while growing up in the northeastern United States. Over five thousand miles of separation had been gobbled up by a short—if not overproduced—verse and chorus. The only thing missing was a mullet flowing down the back of the vendor's neck.

My senses started to pull in whatever else they found. The vendor poured change into the hand of a woman who had bought a copy of the daily *La República* while he chirped *"ta?"*—the hyper-abbreviated Uruguayan Spanish phrase meaning "OK?" He then returned to sipping mate tea from a gourd with a metal, reed-like straw. Ringlets of smoke from a nearby sausage cart wrapped around me, reminding me that the word *vegano* (vegan) had been spray-painted on the façade of a 100-year-old building a few blocks down in reaction to the country's tradition of grilling copious quantities of meat. It also reminded me how the city's vocal authors of graffiti will often risk defacing a landmark to score high visibility for political and societal discourse. The sense of place grew inconveniently complex. I had heard a familiar song, but a new, additional context for it had been established. Kind of like finding the same letter in a different alphabet.

Such complexities may be difficult to acknowledge. And they might destroy a romantic image of a place as remaining exotic and untouched. But new complexities nonetheless nail down a unique sense of place: the moment in front of the kiosk could have only happened in Montevideo, only during our current generation. Such discoveries, for me, demonstrate how large and mutable the world has become.

I grew up in this era of globalization, but Paul Theroux, who has been writing about his travels since I was barely old enough to walk, recently wrote a piece for *Newsweek* (ironically titled "Dispatch from a Shrinking Planet") in which he reflects on the challenges spawned by a more connected world. "These very alterations in culture," he writes, "far from diminishing curiosity, have made much of the world less predictable, more dramatic and accessible, full of paradoxes that have to be seen to be believed."

When I consider the Western Hemisphere, I am reminded that it may still have an additional misconception working against its size. Growing up in the States, I can't forget that until a short time ago, the whole hemisphere had been considered to be under the sphere of influence of Washington, according to the Monroe Doctrine—and its defenders. They claimed that the doctrine was self-evident. Perhaps some still believe it. It's all America's backyard, right? Such a belief lends itself to nice, neat reductionism, another flavor of the shrinking world philosophy.

Somewhere along the way, some folks from the States even commandeered the word "American" to refer only to ourselves. How rude! Even so, I still find myself using the term (like in the previous paragraph). I guess that proves my point (the dominant definition, not the rudeness). If you ask Latin Americans for the definition of American, however, they will tell you that an American is anyone from the Americas, whether Chilean, Honduran, Canadian, Trinidadian—not just someone from the United States.

Eleven years ago, when I began writing my first book, *Is There a Hole in the Boat? Tales of Travel in Panama Without a Car*, I started to concentrate most of my travels in the Western Hemisphere, owing to the freefalling dollar suggesting said region. That was when I found myself traveling as an American in the much broader Latin American sense, as part of the whole. Such a mindset became strengthened when I ended up with a pocketful of pay toilet receipts from Ecuador, printed in blocky, Wild West fonts; or when I spotted a satellite dish sprouting from a thatch roof in a

Guna village in Panama; or when I discussed a recipe for seal flipper pie with a butcher in Quebec City. The lands ended up spawning new questions. To travel is to accept uncertainty.

In venturing to lands near my own, I experienced their largeness—that is, their richness, their deepness, their color, and their resistance to reduction. I feel as if the land has grown a new dimension. The stories in this collection are the result of those travels.

Travel, in another sense, does make the world shrink, however. Travel has the effect of shrinking the world we thought we knew before having traveled—the images of how a place should look and feel, the flimsy placeholders our minds love to create. Several years ago, I had to concede that uncovering unexpected facets of a locale through travel could be possible even in what I had viewed as the most placeless place on earth, the suburb. I had always thought of the suburbs as cultural purgatory; between the city and the country, the suburb boasts none of the benefits of either, while burdened with some of the disadvantages of both.

Thus, I had thought I'd never consider writing a piece that took place in a suburb. My research into New Orleans' gastronomy changed all that, eventually leading me to explore the current state of the city's nutria invasion that has reached the city's borders. "Showdown at the West Esplanade Canal," set completely in the suburbs of the city, went on to win a silver medal in the 2010 Solas Awards. You'll find the piece in this collection.

Throughout the following pages, you won't find any timeless, magical Pan-American connection that binds together an entire hemisphere. Except, perhaps, an emphasis of an alternate definition for the word American. But you'll encounter connections between social electricity and rusty automobile carcasses ("A Dialog of Echoes"), between deep-sea life and toilet bowls ("A Planet Within a Planet"), and between English-language textbooks and the wisdom of drunkards ("Rock Hotel Hospitality"). You'll even find a couple of tales that resulted from travels around my own backyard of New York City, since I don't feel one's own hometown should be exempt from discovery and reflection. New York City is part of the whole that is the Americas.

This book is not meant to serve as a guidebook nor as a blow-by-blow record of all my travels in the Americas. Rather, I chose to focus on the depth of thirty-two encounters across fourteen countries. Each experience has given me an understanding of the cultural dynamics at work. The stories, covering a span of seven years starting in 2004, do not always follow in chronological order, and some names have been changed for reasons of privacy. But together, all have helped define what distance means to me—or doesn't—and how travel has the capability to warp it, shrink it, stretch it, render it abstract or even absurd.

And you don't even have to be partial to Foreigner's biggest hit. I've never really been a huge fan myself, but given the song's ability to travel more than I will in a lifetime—while touching and influencing an uncountable populace in uncountable ways—I have to give it a nod of respect.

Darrin DuFord
March 2016

No Factory, Just People

"In Region Six, donkeys outnumber cows on the thoroughfares," read a recent article on traffic accidents in the *Kaieteur News*, one of Guyana's daily newspapers. Such is the anxious awareness about stray livestock roaming the paved arteries of Region Six, better known as East Berbice-Corentyne, that the animals are seen to have their own pecking order as to who owns the road. Cows? Donkeys? What happened to cars?

I was sitting in one of those marginalized vehicles, a factory-new Toyota, and we had just crossed into East Berbice and followed the coast through a green, humid flatness of rice and cane fields. It was the region's only main road. Sitting next to me in the backseat was Junior, a cab driver I'd been using for the past week on trips around the fading Victorian houses of Georgetown, Guyana's capital city. The tips of his gold teeth peeked from between his relaxed lips. The night before, he and I had been walking along

Georgetown's concrete miles-long seawall, the city's largest weekly hangout, when he ran into a friend, Henry, a Berbice native now living in Georgetown, who invited us to accompany him to the town where he was raised.

Denise, a Trinidadian friend of Henry whom he'd met in college in the States a couple of years ago, sat in the front next to him. She was one of the few vacationers I had met in Guyana, her camera full of pictures and video from her flyover the day before of Kaieteur Falls, the destination most pushed by Guyana's fledgling tourism industry. "The world's tallest single-drop waterfall," echoes the hopeful chant of tourist agencies.

No such chant exists for the coastal stretch of East Berbice. Over a hundred miles from the mountainous, waterfall-rich interior, the landscape that extended before us resembled other rural swatches of coastal Guyana, one of above-ground cemeteries with weathered tombs positioned like ruins of an old temple's foundation; narrow concrete bridges; and impromptu junkyards stacked with gnarled, dismembered chunks of rusted vehicles from bygone manufacturers. Instances of the snackette, the Guyanese mini lunch kiosk, appeared regularly, always named something like Nicky's or Spready's or Shantah's. We passed a husk of a deceased movie theater, its letters having faded into ghostly shapes on its facade. It was killed, as Henry was quick to point out, by the availability of pirated DVDs. "Why pay for theater tickets when the whole family can watch a movie for two dollars?" he asked, laying down a challenge that demonstrated how Guyana and copyright enforcement are far from being acquainted.

The air-conditioning detached us from the coastline's brain-sucking humidity that grips everyone and everything like a mad plague. Cane stalks, however, yearn for such an environment. That was why the Dutch and the English had carved up this flattened lip of South America and unloaded ships full of slaves upon it. Almost two centuries have passed since slavery was abolished in Guyana, yet the geographical legacy of the plantations—each one a thin, rectangular plot bordering the road on its narrow side—remains because each plantation became a separate town, their signs spaced barely a few hundred meters apart from one another. Henry's penchant for pedal stomping enhanced the effect of their closeness.

And then there were the animals. Chickens, donkeys, stray dogs, cows, sheep, sometimes a traffic jam of several species. They grazed on the narrow strip between the curbless roadside and the drainage canals, or moseyed down the center of the road to avoid having to navigate around front yard fences. Still others just stood on the pavement in self-assured poses. *Honk if you think I'm tasty.*

But something else—a heftier, less appealing beast—prowls the roads of Berbice, a beast too rare to appear anywhere else in the world, even too rare for any other part of Guyana. "That's a Tapir," Henry announced without turning around, playing the part of the unflappably calm tour guide, as we passed the first specimen of said thing in the other lane. You might be imagining the porcine-looking creature with a snout so dexterous, the creature can use it to grab its lunch off bushes. But you'd be wrong. The Guyanese named a car, the only car ever built in Guyana, after the aforementioned mammal of the country's interior.

With a boxy, ribbed shell sitting atop undersized wheels—the back tires smaller than the front—the vehicle could be an abandoned lovechild of a go-kart and a shipping container. The designers of the gas-powered, jeep-sized Tapir seemed to have been inspired by the animal's bulk but left out its grace. Perhaps a slicker model may be making its way down the assembly line? I wanted to talk with the designers themselves. "Where is the factory that makes them?" I asked Henry.

"No factory," Henry boomed. "Just people."

He let the answer stand tantalizingly unpacked for a moment. I looked to Junior, the only other Guyanese in the vehicle, but he remained quiet and free of quizzical grimaces. Henry continued, explaining how a prospective owner of a Tapir would order the pieces and assemble them himself, probably in his driveway. Add an ostentatious paint job and some mock bullet-hole adhesives, and another Tapir is born to take back the road from livestock.

A bright pink Tapir rolled by, a grotesque jam of people hunching inside, overlapping, pressing up against the windows like pickles in a jar. The Tapir is Berbice's workhorse of public transportation, even though it is not tall enough to transport seated people in its enclosed cargo space. That's because it was never designed for transporting people. Tapirs were first built in the 1960s and 1970s during the administrations of a left-leaning government eager to cheaply and rapidly construct vehicles to transport goods. Years later, someone looking to extract more profit out of the Tapir introduced the idea that people are cargo too. (And with it, the era of capitalism in independent Guyana had begun.) And here's a bonus: Unlike rigid objects that will break if stuffed into the low-clearance cargo bed, humans can tuck in their gangly heads. Wow, cargo that can pack itself!

"It's the only car ever made in Guyana. And it shows," Henry added, drawing out the word *shows*.

"What do you mean by 'it shows'?" I asked innocently because I really didn't know.

"It's..." started Henry. He seized up, as if barbed memories had interrupted him, had attempted to hijack his larynx, had threatened to force him to utter something too raw for company he had just met the day before. And then, calmly, he said, "It's a machine. Communism 101."

Meanwhile, we had just reached the extreme eastern edge of coastal Guyana. The stores and houses of the riverfront towns (each town about as wide as a few football fields) clung to the road, the only artery connecting them to each other and to the capital. Bootleg DVD emporiums and clothing stores specializing in American brands occupied the first floors of two-story houses. Most of the establishments hung hand-painted signage—their cheerful letters echoing styles that fell out of vogue in other countries after the 1950s—that seemed to slow down the pace of the sheep, the Tapirs, and the sweating humanity all timesharing that skinny spine of pavement.

But we would not stop here to meet Henry's cousin at his riverfront house, as Henry had planned. Not just yet. First, Henry wanted to show us the end of the road, where a ferry dock offered a view across the Corentyne River to Surinam, where we might catch a river breeze to blow away some of the noontime heat. The Tapirs disappeared as we probed deeper southward alongside cane fields. We encountered a prune-faced woman squatting on a concrete sluice gate, dangling a fishing rod into the murk of the canal below, nodding us over to show us her bucket of tiger fish she had caught. I asked her how she managed to catch anything at all from the seemingly inhospitable opaqueness. Her bronze cheeks stretched along well-defined wrinkles into a smile. "Patience," she answered.

Both daily ferries having already left for Surinam, the dock was peaceful, only slightly breezy, and only mildly interesting. A few minutes' worth of lingering proved sufficient for satisfying both the curiosity of us visitors and Henry's memories, so we returned to the car and waited for the gift of air conditioning to bless us. That was when Henry began a slow, repetitive chant: "Oh no...Oh no..."

The car started, but the dashboard remained dark. A fuse had blown. Which meant, in this age of technological conveniences, not only had we lost the air conditioning, but also the windows could not be opened. Manual window cranks? What kind of hopeless Luddite would need those anymore?

The four of us rose out of the car. We chose the raw sun over the oven-like metal and glass of the Toyota. Henry called his cousin. At the lonely pier at the dead end of the road, horror had decided to join our outing, invading Denise's vacation, appropriating Henry's nostalgia, prodding me to quietly estimate the walking time to town. Junior, his light frame hunched as he stood, wore the same mildly curious expression as when he'd been telling me stories of Georgetown's almost daily power outages giving way to the rattle of generators.

The cousin connected Henry with a mechanic. With town about ten miles away, Henry estimated that we could drive for about five minutes at a time with the doors closed, then we'd stop and open the doors, and repeat until we arrived at the mechanic's place. I counted in my head as our first doors-closed session began and Henry stomped on the gas pedal, gunning for the town. The crouching fisherwoman passed in a blur of skin and dirty shorts, and the taste of hot air soured my tongue. Sweat began to sprout from every part of my body as if I were being squeezed. A sharp brake agitated red dust; wet arms shoved open the doors. We had not lasted even a minute. Denise smirked and commented, "How nice to receive an unexpected sauna treatment without having to visit the spa."

By the time we entered town, we had become adept at rolling through our open-door breaks instead of stopping. We needed one last break, but a squad of Tapirs approached in the other lane. There was no shoulder or curb, so we popped open all four doors a few inches to let in life-giving air, along with a stream of nervous honks.

In front of the mechanic's house, Junior and the mechanic were busy digging their hands into the engine, their fingers streaked with black dust. Curious goats trotted by. Henry went in search of a replacement fuse up the road. Behind us, Henry's cousin, who had just parked his car, waved us over and offered air conditioning to any of us that wanted it.

The pointing and fiddling arms of Junior and the mechanic left no room for anyone else near the fuse box, so Denise and I indulged in the cousin's offer. He was a portly man who filled out the driver's seat, and he assured us in a singsong Indo-Guyanese voice that there were no worries—he could have met us at the ferry dock if the car had died completely, or if we had not decided to test the science behind a motor vehicle's greenhouse effect.

A baby-blue Tapir cruised by, trolling for fleshy cargo, its bass-heavy dancehall track shaking the cousin's car.

When I had asked him about the prevalence of Tapirs in Berbice, his words hardened: "Whoever designed those things should be executed." That was the closest I had seen him come to allowing a touch of disgust to crinkle his face.

While waiting for the fuse to arrive, I wandered down the road, spying the groups of sheep staring down approaching traffic and ignoring horns. A Tapir had stopped across from me, its side door opening to reveal it had been fitted with a brass deadbolt lock, the kind found inside the front door of a house. The wedge-shaped hinges had been cannibalized, apparently, from an old footlocker. As with all Tapirs, a government-issued decal stating HACKNEY CARRIAGE 7 SEATS—declaring the vehicle's maximum capacity of one passenger in the front, six in the cargo hold—had been affixed to its back. Yet when the driver opened the cargo door, a stream of bent-up humans kept crawling out, like from a clown car in the circus.

Throughout my travels, I have had some of my most memorable conversations on public transportation, as the equalizing effect of close-quarters transport lends itself to a mutual respect and understanding, regardless of culture or background. But because I had met Henry, I no longer needed to rely on public transit in Berbice.

And then, a chance I could not refuse. Three men leaned against a wall facing a driveway where a sky-blue Tapir was parked, its back door opened to the street in an enticing invitation. One man was wiping his hand on a grease rag. They stopped talking when they noticed me noticing the Tapir. A wave of the rag beckoned me in.

I found myself ducking inside the cargo hold, its walls as thick as—well, a shipping container. I sat up on the padded bench, across from where 2 BLESSED 2 B STRESSED had been painted on the inside wall and—ow! The Tapir wasn't moving, and I had already struck my head. Several fiberglass ribs protruded from the roof, one rib atop each bench, lined up perfectly and sadistically with riders' noggins. Ducking down, I ran my finger over hand-welded corners and speakers mounted by the bases of the benches. The top of the windshield read WANTED in stretched letters. A new Toyota steering wheel had been fitted into a dashboard that sprouted tufts of crusty brown foam. Shards of respect, revulsion, and pity fueled my fascination as I was free to examine the Tapir in all its layers without risking a concussion. I had caught a Tapir as it napped.

Then I noticed the windows. To open one, you slide the Plexiglas with your hand. What had happened to us that afternoon, being sealed airtight into a late model luxury Japanese car, would never have happened in a Tapir. Could never happen. Its crudeness rendered it immune to such a modern technological malady. The hammer of irony knocked my head harder than when I had hit the roof.

"You like it? It's tough," said one of the men, his nest of a beard quivering as he thumped the side panel with his meaty fist. He owned the beast, drove it, and maintained it with his brother, the stocky fellow with the rag. He reached under one of the benches and produced a plastic liter bottle of bright yellow liquid. "Extra gas in case it runs out," he added.

I asked him how old the frame was. He turned to the others. They agreed on a number: "Forty years." A decade older than any of them.

As if they had seen slight, upturned lines of approval in my face when I examined the vehicle—and perhaps they were right—his brother barked, "They tip over."

The Tapir, a perplexing artifact from an ideological age, remains in Berbice, a well-maintained town with freshly painted houses and ample foot (and hoof) traffic, while much more modern taxis, meant to transport people, traverse the rest of Guyana, even in the most gruesome, disadvantaged corners of the country. The Tapir not only survives, but it is encouraged and cultivated with paint jobs, sunroofs, spoilers, and bare-breasted hood ornaments—each serving as an extension of its owner's personality and hubris. The Tapir is the drunken uncle who embarrasses kin at family get-togethers, eliciting rebukes, causing shame, but in the end, is still part of the family.

Smiles reappeared around Henry's car. Success. Next stop: belated lunch at one of his favorite restaurants, one of the original points of interest in Henry's itinerary. But after seating ourselves in plastic chairs around a table in an empty dining room, we learned that we had arrived at the eatery so late that the cook had run out of everything but roast chicken over fried rice. We all ordered it. Henry pandered to his nostalgia and opted for a Crown Spot Lemonade—like the Tapir, made in Berbice. He chose not to describe it in terms of how it tasted better, sweeter, or tarter than other lemonades; holding up the squat bottle with lettering as anachronistic as the hand-painted signs from roadside stores, Henry said, "You can get it only in Berbice." He had fixed his eyes outward to no point in particular, following the threads of whatever memories had been stirred up.

A few houses away, his cousin invited us to walk through his yard, past his fruit trees, to the riverside, where a decaying pier poked into the river. Henry, Denise, and Junior carefully stepped over the missing planks for an irresistible photo op, while I walked with his cousin along the river's edge. "Here, life is relaxed," he said to me as waves tenderly slapped the pier's posts. He explained how the piers along the town's coast host canoes and other small boats that can take passengers across to Surinam illegally, a practice called backtracking. "It's very common here," he said. The piers saw much more action than the legal crossing we had visited earlier. Police board the illegal motorboats about as often as copyright police arrest vendors of illegally copied DVDs, or about as often as owners of livestock reign in their cows and sheep from the road.

We followed a line of litter, along the coast by the pier, pushed up by the waves: cigarette boxes, water bottles, moldy shoes, a box with Dutch wording from bakeries with Surinamese addresses, the latter recently discarded by a backtracker with a sweet tooth. I wondered if the Surinamese ginger beer I had drunk at the restaurant had arrived legally or illegally.

"Life is relaxed, unless, of course, you get sick," the cousin continued. "There's no health care this far out. If you're sick, you have to go to Georgetown." One hundred miles away.

I asked him why there was no hospital here. He swatted the air. "Here, life is cheap." Within a minute, a fascinating pairing—life is relaxed; life is cheap. Relaxed enough to avoid the hassle of regulation; cheap enough to be treated like a sack of rice in the back of a Tapir. I found it an unwieldy balance, but also one that exposes beads of societal glue that keep the DVD stores stocked, the fried rice flavored with star anise sauce, the forty-year-old Tapir engines running, the backtracking vessels smuggling.

The day began to lose its heat. Henry indicated that we should head back to Georgetown because after sundown, the cows like to sleep on the road—the nine-hundred-pound jaywalkers turn into squatters—excitingly elevating the challenges of Berbice driving.

Fading shafts of low sun gilded the cane fields in metallic orange. It was not bovine bedtime, not yet. One cow lumbered along the center of the road, no doubt tired after a hectic day of roadside grazing, forcing Henry to creep along to avoid hitting her. I could have poked her bony shoulder from the open car window. Her bulging eye kept staring ahead in a Zen-like detachment, the creature not knowing that she is a hazard that could fell Tapir and imported luxury sedan alike, not knowing that such a savage strike will result in mutually assured destruction. The bovine version of the balance of life in Berbice.

Journey by Bottle

Raw cassava juice is so toxic that six ounces can kill a man. Yet when the juice is boiled down, its poison is destroyed and the liquid becomes cassareep, a black, bittersweet syrup—one of Guyana's most popular flavoring sauces. It's a reality that, with any justice, would allow cassava juice to eclipse the international fame of that other poisonous liquid from Guyana, Jim Jones' vintage 1978 Kool-Aid.

When I arrived in Guyana, I could not detect a single whiff of fascination for the whole Jonestown massacre thing. Refreshing. Instead, cassareep stood proud and unchallenged, turning up in steam-table fried rice, in stews at sit-down restaurants, on grocery store shelves next to machetes, and in reused beer bottles in the markets of Georgetown, the capital. A sauce company's billboard displaying a giant bottle of cassareep even flanks the entrance to Georgetown from the airport road, getting me coming and going.

Considering such prevalence, I am not surprised that cassareep is the linchpin ingredient in the country's national dish, pepperpot, a stew of sweet, oil-black broth from which the diner fishes for assorted pieces of on-the-bone goat, lamb, beef, or whatever other meat the cook has procured. The cuts could be anything from brisket to salted pig's tails to cow heels. I learned fast that Guyana is a country that doesn't require a gastronomic nose-to-tail movement to venture—often—into the gelatinous realm of heels and trotters, and that cassareep complements it all.

After days of being haunted by the versatile flavoring sauce—sometimes smoky, sometimes barky, always with a viscous, molasses-like body—I wished to uncover its origins. I hit pay dirt at Annai, population 512, a village of Makushi Amerindians in the sweaty savannah of southern Guyana. Approaching Annai's dirt runway in a Trans-Guyana Airways Cessna, I saw a tiny enclave of humanity coming into view: on one side of the strip, a few dozen thatched-roof houses huddled on a low hill; the Rock View Lodge, an ecolodge run by a British expat, stood a few dozen steps from the runway on the other side. At the lodge, I met Leon, a young, relaxed guide, who held up a cylindrical basket made of straw, about a meter long with a coarse, diagonal weave as tight as that of a straw hat. A thick loop was woven to each end. This device was a matapee, the Amerindian tool that, when filled with shredded cassava, yields the raw juice used for cassareep.

I found its tubular shape curious; Leon told me that, according to Amerindian legend, the matapee owes its design to the gruesome table manners of a carnivorous reptile: the anaconda. Leon explained through exaggerated gestures how the tool, when stuffed with cassava that has been shredded on a nail-studded board, squeezes the cassava in the same way that a snake elongates itself to squeeze the prey it has just swallowed. The narrow gaps in the matapee's weave allow the juice to run out; it's then boiled down ("Yeh bile it doan" in Leon's Guyanese English) to destroy the cyanide. After the addition of spices such as cinnamon and habanero pepper, the black liquid becomes cassareep. As a bonus, the dry solids left inside can be scooped out and used as flour for baking.

To demonstrate proper matapee stretching technique, Leon hooked one loop of the empty matapee to the post of a thatched-roof house, and wrapped both hands around the other loop. He had attended school in the more populated coastal region of Guyana, but as with many Guyanese I would meet in urban and rural areas alike, he still knew how to use the matapee. It seemed to me to be some sort of cultural litmus test. "You have to keep your chickens away when doing this," he said as he leaned forward, away from the post, leveraging his weight to stretch the matapee. "If they eat raw cassava, they will die."

It remains unclear how the Amerindians first discovered that if cassava juice is boiled, it is not only safe to consume, but also makes a savory sauce. It's safe to say that the cooks who got it wrong ended up paralyzing themselves and their guests before being able to pass on their recipes. The practice of cultivating and then meticulously processing a tuber dripping with the juice of death may appear labor-intensive (if not mildly insane), but the Makushi and other Amerindian nations of the savannah have favored cassava because it takes well to poor tropical soil, the soil to which cassava has adapted since before humans began cultivating it. They call upon cassava for many culinary uses—bread, cakes, farofa (toasted cassava flour), and cassareep, building on their tradition of cultivating cassava that reaches back at least 10,000 years. The Amerindians invented not only cassareep, but also pepperpot. In modern times, descendants of former slaves and servants from England's colonial rule of Guyana (South America's only English-speaking country) have embraced the dish as their own, and now make their own cassareep, correctly pronounced in Guyana's Caribbean-influenced accent as CAH-zuh-rip.

While squeezing another use out of cassava helped to extend the value of the crop, the Amerindians probably kept making cassareep in part because it demonstrated a special talent. When added to a stew, it keeps meat from spoiling, even in the merciless heat of the savannah, as long as the pot is reheated to a boil once per day—a handy quality-of-life booster in the era before refrigeration. The cook only needs to add more cassareep to the pot when more meat is added. There have been several documented cases of pepperpots lasting for years, like a continuously fed sourdough starter, their flavors becoming marvelously complex.

Not everyone takes advantage of this property. Offering his preferred use for leftover pepperpot, Leon said—in a low voice, as if he were making a confession—"One of my favorites is the pepperpot cheese sandwich."

I stepped into the village's general store, a concrete, barracks-style building near the airstrip. Despite the village's geographic isolation—Annai lies 300 miles from Georgetown down an unpaved highway that floods in the summer—globalization has arrived on the store's shelves in the form of Chinese-made baby clothing and Del Monte vegetables, among other items. Yet next to a shelf of Oreos, cooking oil, and whatever other packaged goods arrive down the highway, I noticed a row of Annai's own cassareep in reused rum bottles. I walked over to the village's community center, where I found a wall covered with several hand-written poems that had won a recent talent contest, one piece containing such considerations as "I am a young and talented Makushi beauty / Fishing and farming is my way of life / Eating pepperpot makes me feel strong and healthy." In Annai, I doubt Worcestershire sauce will be dethroning cassareep any time soon.

When I returned to Georgetown, each bottled goods vendor at the zinc-covered Bourda Market gave me her own distinctly opinionated pepperpot recipe over the distorted rumble of dancehall reggae and chutney CDs from nearby stalls. Several vendors commanded me to add cinnamon and nutmeg. Another, between relating stories of her two sons who work as taxi drivers in Brooklyn, New York, told me I could not make pepperpot without a "stick of thyme." A nearby butcher shop accommodated the breadth of its customers' tastes by listing several popular pepperpot combinations on a chalkboard, each including the likes of cow heels, lamb shanks, or pork butt.

No matter the recipe, the dish spans Guyana's occasionally thorny ethnic divides. For several centuries, the Amerindians of Guyana have had to reckon with the imposing ethnic legacy left behind from England's colonial rule of Guyana—descendants of slaves who worked the coastal cane fields, and descendants of indentured servants brought from India when slavery was abolished. Together, the two latter groups account for ninety percent of Guyana's population. The Indo-Guyanese, the Afro-Guyanese, and the Amerindians do not always agree politically, as each ethnic group has tended to vote with parties comprised more or less of their own stripe. But pepperpot has become both a stew pot and a melting pot, its earthy, bittersweet flavor earning a universal appreciation.

Using nail boards and matapees can provide a family, or even a small village, with enough cassareep to keep their pepperpots alive longer than the village elders. But how can the country produce enough cassareep to meet the needs of the nation's 750,000 people, especially at Christmastime, when the dish serves as a traditional, secular holiday meal all across the religious spectrum, even for the country's Hindus and Muslims?

I crossed the floating bridge over the Demerara River from Georgetown to the flat cropland of La Grange, where I met with Ram Prashad, owner of Prestige Foods, at the company's bottling factory. Varnished shelves in the office foyer displayed sample bottles of his goods—mango achar, bitter gourd in lime sauce, and of course cassareep. A plastic figurine of Ganesh, the elephant-headed Hindu deity of knowledge and wisdom, sat cross-legged among the bottles and kept watch.

I caught Ram at a demanding time. It was two weeks before Christmas. He pointed out that his factory, its buildings reaching back railroad-style into a narrow, deep lot, was producing twice the usual amount of cassareep to answer the nation's seasonal demand. Over the clatter of recycled Coca-Cola crates moving across rollers, he explained that only one percent of his cassava extract currently originates from Amerindian communities like Annai, the rest arriving from family-owned factories that use spiked wheels to grate cassava faster than can be achieved with a nail board.

Despite the cassava going through a partially mechanized process, Ram still wants to maintain the homemade flavor of cassareep with which all Guyanese have grown up. "My goal is to keep products in the purest state," he said. Referring to American-made packaged foods, he remarked, "I can't pronounce some of the names of the ingredients."

The flavor of cassareep, according to Ram, develops from its preparation techniques just as much as its ingredient list. When I asked him if he could elaborate, he quickly answered, "It doesn't matter if I tell you. You still can't make it." He did, however, suggest that the sauce tastes best when simmered over a hardwood fire, and sure enough, his cassareep possesses a gentle smokiness that others do not.

When he walked me to the open-walled bottling area in back, I found one of the ingredients piled on a ten-foot table: habaneros. Green, orange, and red. Thousands of them. Some were destined for cassareep, and the rest would end up in hot sauce.

Just as Ram tailors his bottled products to Guyanese palates, he has adapted his factory to the temperament of the Guyanese power grid and its daily power outages. He brought me to the plant's outdoor area, which is only covered by a roof, and pointed to a meter-deep, funnel-shaped vessel filled with hot sauce. "I built this myself," Ram said, not proudly but matter-of-factly. The device uses gravity and a valve to allow a single factory worker to fill bottles one by one. If—make that when—a power outage strikes, his factory can keep bottling until he runs out of sauce.

The wisdom of the building's open walls soon became evident. The barbed scent of the ever-eager crushed habaneros had no trouble finding my nostrils despite the light breezes from the river refreshing the air. "If you don't make this outdoors," Ram warned, "you're in trouble, mon."

Owing to such dauntless manufacturing, cassareep is found in all ten administrative regions of Guyana and is exported to wherever Guyanese have settled around the world, including Region 11, the name the Guyanese have affectionately given to New York City, home to 130,000 Guyanese-Americans. No matter where they have settled, Guyanese can make pepperpot without the inconveniences of nail boards and poisoned chickens.

Since my return from Guyana I have burned through all the cassareep I brought home to New York, spurring repeat visits to the Guyanese grocery stores along Liberty Avenue in South Richmond Hill, Queens. In the resourceful spirit of the Guyanese, I have discovered how well cassareep adds a smoky body to baked beans. When mixed with passion fruit concentrate, agave syrup, and crushed hot peppers, cassareep creates a spicy-sweet barbecue sauce that pork ribs seem to beg for. That cassareep uncannily dovetails with some classic American dishes means you don't have to be down for gelatinous cow heels to try it.

But cassareep does not conquer every culinary challenge. I have yet to score success creating a cassareep-based dish with vegetables alone. (Even my baked beans needed some bacon to meet the approval of the cassareep.) I can already hear the jeers coming from Georgetown in response to my futile attempts to shut out meat, cassareep's soul mate.

While cassareep may be far from becoming a culinary ingredient du jour in the States, it has become a victim of its own popularity among Guyanese. Knockoff cassareep is now manufactured in Costa Rica, Thailand, and other countries, yet still marketed as a genuine Guyanese product. Always check the label. I scan for "Product of Guyana" before I buy, a task that reminds me very enjoyably of the markets of Guyana, where the crowded stalls drew me closer to the habaneros and the matapees and the thumping dancehall reggae that gently shakes every bottle.

The Search for the Golden Fleece

For a moment, I could have been a treasure hunter who had just landed in the New World. I was grabbing chunks of rich, on-the-bone meat from a helping of labba (known as paca in parts of Latin America), a cat-size rodent caught in the wilderness nearby, while a weak trade wind attempted to push away clots of ninety-five-degree air. A map lay open before me.

But instead of a parrot on my shoulder, I turned and met with the hunched figure of an albino salesman attempting to unload pirated DVDs. "You like *Transformers?*" he chirped.

I was sitting in an open-air restaurant in Parika, Guyana, enjoying the aforementioned local specialty, which had been slow-stewed with orange peel and garlic. The treasure I sought was neither gold nor computer-generated Decepticons. It was something I'd spotted on the map of the other side of the nearby Essequibo River: a town named Golden Fleece.

Guyana boasts a bounty of unforgettable place names, chalking up festive roadside specimens such as Bee Hive, Now or Never, Vryheid's Lust, and Zorg. Many are legacies of slave-run plantations from the days of Dutch and British colonial rule.

But Golden Fleece?

I was reminded of the story of the ancient order of the same name, whose insignia was, allegedly, a lock from a prince's favored fair-haired lady. The term has also been used poetically to describe women with blonde hair. Above all, the name struck me because blonde hair in Guyana is almost as rare as snowfall—give or take an albino DVD salesman.

I had to visit.

The car-carrying ferry traversing the milk-chocolatey river would not be leaving for hours. But after filling up Weson (my taxi driver) with labba, I persuaded him to strap on a life jacket and accompany me on the faster option: a roofless water taxi that zigzagged around mangrove-stran-gled islands in the river's mouth. When we reached the other side, we took a cab into farmland dotted with wooden houses bleached to a pale gray from the sun. Rice fields stretched out to our west; the Atlantic Ocean slapped the concrete seawall behind the houses to our east.

A hulking rice mill and a cemetery announced the town. No plaza, no center. Near the cemetery stood a zinc-roofed, Anglican house of worship, the church of Golden Fleece, and I tried not to consider its metaphorical implications.

Instead, I began looking for someone we could shake down for a history lesson. The owner of a nearby video game store, seated behind a glass case filled with squares of color-copied packaging, aimed wide, puzzled eyes at us when I asked him how the town had acquired its name.

"I've lived here all my life, an' I don' know," he confessed. Then again, if a stranger walked into my stomping grounds of Oxford, Connecticut, and asked me who had named it, and where he might find the oxen, I might be a bit puzzled too.

A passing bicyclist quickly answered, "The Dutch named it," as if we should have known. Golden Fleece didn't sound exceedingly Dutch to me, although the Dutch seemed suitable donors of this recessive gene, the legacy of which remained at large.

Near the road, a scruffy sheep on a leash stretched its neck to bite a clump of grass. Its coat was matted, but marginally goldenish. Perhaps I should have given more attention to livestock, not people. Do the Guyanese prize this wool? When I heard myself ask Weson, I knew the question was daft—ninety-five degrees and all.

"We eat dem. We throw away deh wool," he said, gesturing in the same snapping motion I'd seen him use when tossing an empty soda bottle out the taxi window.

We walked farther down to an open patio of a bar with a sign by the door: NO CREDIT, DON'T ASK US. I bought the only nonalcoholic drink available, some Mystic carrot juice blend, and approached a table of three pink-eyed men in tank tops. Three toothy grins flashed. I hoped their friendliness indicated a willingness to chat. Weson became restless, a warning sign I did not heed.

They were certainly willing to chat, asking where I was from while having me photograph their best thumbs-up poses. Again and again. The men didn't seem interested in answering my question, and instead, one insisted on pouring rum into my Mystic bottle. Weson, knowing that the only knowledge I'd gain was that carrot juice and rum make a nasty cocktail, ushered me out. The secret of Guyana's Golden Fleece, if one exists, appears to be safe with them.

We seemed to have exhausted the town's entire population. English is the official language of Guyana, but I still felt as if something had become lost in translation.

Returning to Parika, we passed a town named Adventure. No need to uncover its origins.

A Dialog of Echoes

Diesel smoke, grill smoke, cigarette smoke. They were just warm-ups for a face full of fumes from burning cardboard and furniture. At the curb, I stood over the flames, too enchanted to seek fresher air. A burly Iranian man urged me to draw from a soda bottle refilled with red wine as a girl I had never met greeted me with a kiss on the cheek.

It was Friday night in Montevideo, Uruguay, and I was waiting for the *candombe* drum group Tambor Brujo to begin its weekly march through otherwise quiet streets. Over a dozen drummers had placed their drums sideways around the fire so the heat would tune up the horsehide heads. "It's like Jimi Hendrix," a scruffily bearded drummer commented to me when he threw a newspaper into the fire. Unlike Hendrix's guitar, the drums themselves remained singe-free, their heads glowing in the firelight like setting suns.

Barrel-shaped and ribbed with metal rings, the candombe drum looks and sounds similar to the conga, since both claim a common origin in the traditions of Bantu peoples of Africa, brought to Uruguay and Cuba as slaves. The group waiting around the fire, however, reflected the ethnic makeup of modern Uruguay: mostly white. Just as blues in America is no longer race specific, so went candombe in Uruguay.

Nor is candombe gender specific. Nor fashion specific. Aside from a few drummers wearing red Tambor Brujo t-shirts, the sartorial hodgepodge espoused Montevideo's standard casual style: cargo shorts, jeans, loafers, flip-flops. Painted drum designs ranged from flames to hammers and sickles. They stood like a ragtag band about to support a ragtag army, without the army.

Tambor Brujo is one of many candombe groups that march through the city's streets. During Carnival, each group, or *cuerda*, dons matching costumes and Day-Glo face paint. But tonight, in mid-March, the idea was just to go out and drum.

I approached Lalo, a drummer who also administers websites for Uruguayan musicians. While he was collecting his instrument from the fire, I asked him if the drums bother the neighbors. Without looking up, he answered, "They're accustomed."

Accustomed. An ominously ambiguous word choice. It could mean that the people have given up, have found some lip-biting way of coping. Many Americans, for example, have become accustomed to their families and friends hunching over iPhones at the dinner table.

When the group began to march and the cracks of sticks striking tight skin began bouncing between façades, I learned what accustomed meant. Flip-flop-wearing residents walked out onto the sidewalk to watch. Toddlers with tyke-sized candombe drums strapped onto them waited in thresholds, egged on by their parents to play along.

Meanwhile, several young women had begun swaying in a hip-whipping dance in front of the drummers, albeit wearing considerably more fabric than during Carnival. People walking their dogs steered their pets alongside the cuerda. Couples circled while snapping photos, the cuerda gaining mass with each block.

I followed the sounds of the drums ricocheting off the houses. The walls seemed alive, responding to the drums in perfect time. As a percussionist, I caught a naughty thrill hearing the irresistibly sweet—and often forbidden—marriage of drums and street acoustics. That was when I noticed Pocitos—this residential neighborhood—was noticeably well kept, showing off its bright window trim and proud, lush trees. I thought of David Byrne's ruminations in his *Bicycle Diaries* concerning the usual correlation between a neighborhood's affordability and its tolerance for eccentricity. I wished he could have joined us, bike and all. As a side benefit of choosing a pleasant urban neighborhood for drumming, there's a steady supply of slightly used, discarded furniture to burn when it comes time to tune up.

The cuerda blocked traffic, forcing cars to crawl at the pace of the synchronized steps. No one honked. No obscene gestures stabbed the air. Some cars refused to remain silent, however, owing to the degree of affluence that ushers in inevitable car alarms. The rumble of bass from the larger drums set the alarms of parked cars a-squealing, that awful robotic blare whose only purpose is to agitate. Shame on those drivers for polluting the street with noise!

Twenty drummers ended their performance on one tight note. The façades busied themselves with echoing applause.

As I fell asleep that night, I kept thinking about the fans—the parents in the thresholds and their kids holding their cool little coffee-can-sized drums.

THE NEXT MORNING, I was still coughing up essence of bourgeois chair leg. Someone was spray-painting a mural on the façade of an art foundation across from my hotel. I had already started a collection of mural photos from previous walks in Montevideo—Batman with a bare, protruding gut; Jesus in tighty-whities; fish with opposable thumbs. The streets were speaking. I kept listening.

I wondered what statement the rusty Studebakers and Morrises along the curb were making. Despite contributing to the city's sooty air, the cars must have been tickling a particular aesthetic fancy. Some were junked, but were somehow entitled to parking spots as their final resting places, where they oxidized in peace; a charming respect for the elderly. It was as if removing them would be an act of vandalism.

Manicured plazas line the city's main avenue, 18 de Julio, at conveniently regular intervals, natural meeting points of which Montevideans take advantage. Young couples nuzzling foreheads, mothers nursing al fresco, a trio in soccer jerseys sharing a gourd of bitter yerba mate tea on a park bench. Texting remained a rare sight.

At this early hour, the drummers had swapped out their instruments for gourds and hot water–filled thermoses as they walked into bakeries or music stores. But their presence lingered. Several murals featured depictions of candombe drumming, past and present. When I asked a tailor if any cuerdas perform in the narrow streets near his Ciudad Vieja storefront, he dropped his scissors, fetched his own drum that he stores in his shop, and dove into an excited description—half verbal, half manual—of his own cuerda, all while someone's pants lay on the table charmingly un-hemmed.

I passed a couple of piles of ashes near the curb, evidence of recent cuerda activity. Back in the States, street drummers—just like roadside car carcasses—would usually be viewed as quality-of-life violations (especially with the public alcohol consumption). I remained intrigued at the cuerda's acceptance in Montevidean society.

It would be the frequency of murals, bustling central plazas, and curb-beautifying Studebakers that would begin to cast light on the popularity of the city's public percussion. And perhaps vice versa. There was an undeniable current of social electricity coursing through the streets of Montevideo, streets serving as destinations that help bond neighbors so they feel they live with the city, not just in it. In those streets, cuerdas—group efforts themselves—were born.

FOR THE PAST WEEK, I'd been in taxis blocked by cuerdas. I'd walked with cuerdas that blocked taxis. But I had yet to experience the music from the drummer's perspective.

I took my first lesson with Tatita Marquez—drummer, composer, and candombe historian—in his studio, located on a stencil-sprinkled block in that apparent contradiction of a neighborhood, middle class Pocitos. He had painted the walls of his studio in alternating colors, reminding me of hues for shag rugs—lime green, Muppet orange. A thicket of drums and mixing boards surrounded us.

Since his college years, he has been fusing candombe with electronic and other forms of music, and has toured on three continents. But for our lesson, he introduced me to the basic street-drumming patterns he grew up with, on all three candombe drums, the *chico*, *repique*, and *piano*—small, medium, and large, respectively. His head shaven, he was all muscle and passion poking out from a tank top. "We start with wood," he said, referring to candombe's characteristic strike of the stick on the drum shell.

The accents took a crisp departure from the downbeat-intensive grooves of my days as a drummer in a punk 'n' roll band some years ago. And I had never used the candombe configuration—one stick and one hand. But what slowly blossomed was an interlocking rhythm between our drums, hitting the same pleasure receptors as when biting into a complex yet well-balanced dish. Each flavor—or rhythm—complements the others in some predetermined, perfected way, the combination of which is greater than the sum of its parts.

The rhythm formed a lively dialog, a food group for social animals. Fittingly, the drum parades during Carnival are called *llamadas*, or calls, as in calling neighbors to join the parade when it passes by.

MANY OF THEM can't stand up by themselves. I'm talking about yerba mate gourds. Since Mother Nature rarely offers us fruit with flat surfaces, the gourds, when dried and fashioned into teacups, need little legs sewn onto them to keep them from falling over. Most Uruguayans have still not forsaken the old-school gourd—kind of like a handheld Studebaker—for something requiring less maintenance.

As I watched the Uruguayans clutching their mate paraphernalia while they climbed into buses, hung out in the city's plazas, or sat in the thresholds of crumbling colonial tenements, it became clear that the awkward portability of the thermos-and-gourd routine should not be mistaken for accessories to a fast-lane lifestyle. The gear is designed to allow the drinker to share tea outside the house and in the social fabric of the streets. The leisurely passing of the legless gourd from friend to friend in front of a manicured fountain seemed to reveal identity much more than inconvenience.

Only a strong sense of identity could keep a Uruguayan gripping his thermos between his arm and chest while dancing in front of a cuerda. The first time I saw this, the metaphorical implications were inescapable: his arm out as if holding a partner, giving the image of a dancing couple, man and thermos, spinning together.

By my last drum lesson, the effect of identity had colored the mood more than the walls of Tatita's studio. He taught me three different but related rhythms that have originated in three neighborhoods. The districts—Barrio Sur, Palermo, Cordón—are close to one another; in a half-hour walk, you could hit them all. But each rhythm has its own feel: the accelerated speed in Cordón, the extra accent on the *chico* in Palermo. Terroir for music.

Tatita was born in Palermo, a neighborhood where Afro-Uruguayans started marching candombe drums through the streets in the 1940s. Apparently, no womb within earshot has been immune to the tug of rhythms that eventually leaped over the walls of racism. I asked the thirty-five-year-old Tatita how long he has been playing; with a confident nod, he answered, "Thirty-five years." Mental picture drawn: a tyke-sized drum strapped onto a tyke-sized Tatita.

The grownup Tatita related stories of how the military dictatorship, from 1973 to 1984, would throw someone in jail for playing drums in the streets, except during a few allowed fiestas. With the return of street drumming, the dialog of candombe rhythms is changing, as all living languages do. Some groups are starting to play different *claves*, or basic rhythm keys. "People prefer the new breaks," he commented. He switched to English, for emphasis, and added, "Some think their candombe died, but it is the evolution of candombe."

If it weren't for evolution, we would have neither tango nor candombe. Both styles find common roots in African rhythms but diverged over a century ago. Tango acquired European instrumentation and melodies, and candombe simplified the clave while becoming the percussive backbone of many Uruguayan jazz and rock recordings.

He offered me a gourd filled to the top with loose tea and water. The metal straw resembled a little oboe reed, preventing the water from being slurped, thus keeping it hot. After one sip, my head felt like a giant tea bag that had been stuffed with freshly mowed grass and oregano, and I had somehow willingly dunked myself in a bucket of hot water. Tatita snickered, not the laughing-with-you kind.

I hesitated. He returned to the same didactic seriousness as when teaching me how to spread my fingers to strike a bass note on the piano. "You have to finish it," he said.

Some facets of Uruguayan identity are more easily understood than others.

SUNDAYS ARE USUALLY CALM in Latin America. Not in Montevideo. Starting at sunrise, the city's largest street market bursts with musty Carlos Gardel LPs, machetes, albino puppies, tomatoes, and thermos-clenching elbows. By late afternoon, the restaurant *parrilladas*—large wood-fired grills—will have seared over a ton of steak. As if refusing to acknowledge that the weekend is ending, Sunday nights are the biggest for cuerdas.

One of the most popular is La Melaza (Molasses in English), an all-female group. While almost every cuerda has at least a few women, the ratio still tips heavily in the direction of men, hence the formation of La Melaza (they do, however, encourage male drummers to join them the last week of each month).

How large is La Melaza? When I approached the dead end where the drums sat around a fire, I asked a young member crouching in comfy sweatpants, her fingers taped up. "Maybe forty this time," she said, "but it depends on who shows up. You can always count the drums."

When the group lined up and began marching, I became part of a throng following the drummers. The fans outnumbered the drummers two to one. I ran into Lalo, who corrected me when he spotted me walking behind the cuerda. Walking? That's a no-no. "Step like this," Lalo commanded, stomping on the quarter notes, so that we all formed one inseparable gust of humanity, together with the thermos dancers, the synchronized hands slapping chico drums, and the occasional fan squatting and pissing in the middle of the street.

Cartons of wine made from Tannat, a grape common in Uruguayan wineries, made their way around. I'm sure there is an interesting story that explains why candombe drums are usually played with just one stick, but a few drummers demonstrated another incentive: You can keep the beat with the stick and still grab a swig from the carton when it comes by.

Uruguayan musician Hugo Fattoruso kicks off the first track of his jazz-candombe album *Emotivo* with a spirited narration of his country's candombe heritage, celebrating candombe's *calor de piel*, or heat of the skin, which can conveniently refer to the drumhead, the hands, or both. As I fielded a carton of Tannat, the buildings locked in said warmth like a blanket, wrapping it around me, around the drummers, around the residents dancing on the balconies. Coming from the often-fragmented social landscape of New York, I was overwhelmed, but also enchanted—comfortably adrift in a people connected to each other, a people connected to a city. A city where drums contribute to the quality of life.

THE WEEK BEFORE I HAD ARRIVED in Montevideo, I met a Uruguayan student outside a sausage cart in Panama City. "I've been living in Panama for three years now, but I still hear the drums in my head every Sunday night," he remarked. A rather romantic statement, I thought. And one that resurfaced when I was in a taxi going to the airport for my departure from Uruguay. The driver handed me some crackers, the most humble of the many edible offerings the Uruguayans had shared with me. Then I realized what I was doing. I was chewing in the rhythm of the clave.

International Avenue

A horse-drawn cart competing with a Toyota Corolla should have been the first thing I noticed. It was an irresistible example of two ages cohabitating. But as I walked onto the median of the widest avenue in Chuy, Uruguay, a different pair of cohabitants had stolen my attention. Fragments of Spanish and Portuguese peppered the thick, moist air, not from different conversations, but from the same, and in the same sentences. The people of Chuy refer to the linguistic mélange as Portuñol, and it was fitting for escorting me off the median, for when I stepped onto the other side, I was in Chuí, Brazil. That would explain the duty-free shops that faced each other across the median.

Chuy—or Chuí—isn't a border town. The town is the border. Shouldn't there at least have been a couple of bored government employees in starched uniforms, sitting at a desk in a booth on the median, asking to see passports? The only customs officers, so I was told by a sidewalk vendor of pirated CDs, sat several blocks from the median, hidden away from all the action. No one has to bother finding them unless one plans on leaving the town limits in either direction. Instead, I was free to roam this overlapping seam of nations, this center of a geographic Venn diagram that seemed to resist my attempts to nail down a singular sense of place.

International brands—Polo, Johnny Walker, Levi—seemed appropriate for lining the avenue, yet the featureless concrete buildings only added to the curious dislocation I had been experiencing. The town had taken generic products of globalization out of an airport's sterile environment and threw them into a sort of benevolent trading post atmosphere, whose streets circulated with bicycles, rusted-out pickups, and the just-noticed horse, pulling a cart, constructed of faded tropical wood, rolling on bald car tires. Meanwhile, sausage carts adorned with multilingual signage, racks of baby onesies made in China, and stacks of *Avatar* DVDs bulged onto the sidewalks, creating impromptu hedges.

The town's dual elements began to appear, however, just a few steps from the avenue. A few moments ago, when I was one block south, I had bought a few Uruguayan *alfajores* at a bakery. After I walked a half block north of the avenue, in Brazil, I entered a grocery store that stocked a dozen brands of Brazilian malagueta pepper sauce. I found the nearness welcoming, and I felt as if I were roaming through different, thriving ethnic neighborhoods of a single city squarely inside a single country.

I reflected on how Chuy's multi-national bustle contrasts with the town's past role as a no man's land. A bastard offspring of colonial paranoia and industrious smuggling,

Chuy grew out of what used to be a buffer zone between the Spanish and Portuguese empires. This no man's land has now become every man's land, a vortex of prices marked in reals and pesos (and sometimes dollars), poking up from the middle of a shorn, flat landscape of cow pastures and lagoons teaming with nutria—furry, voracious, twelve-pound rodents—that have never cared for borders.

I brought a bottle of pepper sauce to the checkout counter. *"Dez'ete"*—seventeen, the cost in Uruguayan pesos—said the unshaven grocery clerk in lazy Portuguese or rapid Spanish or standard Portuñol, I could not tell. But he understood my Spanish, and even answered my question about street directions in kind. Trilingual, he is.

I asked him for the address of a nearby *churrascaria*. I had figured that a solid experience of *espeto corrido*—the uniquely Brazilian style of restaurant where the waiters keep bringing swords full of impaled meat to your table until you capitulate—would help shake off some of my cultural vertigo.

I wasn't the only one waiting for the waiters to take down the FECHADO sign from the door of the Churrascaria La Fortaleza. A broad-shouldered man had been peeking into the window when I began doing the same. Edelmar, an Uruguayan who owns a ranch several miles west of town, had arrived to pick up some duty-free stuffed animals for his kids. "The kids can't wait," he told me, smiling. "They say 'Barney now!'" The tide of cultural vertigo was beginning to envelop me. I decided to surf it and see where it took me.

Edelmar, fluent in Spanish, Portuguese, Portuñol, and English, leaned his thick upper body forward when he spoke, exuding a confidence tempered by his gentle eyes.

He insisted we share a table. I delighted at the prospect of dining with an Uruguayan rancher, and I wondered if the steak I had been eating in Uruguay could have been grazing around his ranch just the week before.

All the waiters recognized him and greeted him with bobbing chins and brows, hinting that his kids boast a rather large stuffed animal collection. Looking forward to practicing English, he translated for me as the meat swords came around, and I recognized the cuts as the same as from the Brazilian restaurants in my Queens neighborhood, starting with sirloin, its juice lasciviously dripping down the spit. Over the beef, Edelmar, whose family tree straddles Uruguay and Brazil like Chuy itself, told me that his wife is a dentist, he owns 4,000 head of cattle, and he insists that he is still middle class by the area's standards.

I mentioned that I was interested in owning a farm someday. Without pausing, he said, "In Uruguay, you don't have to plant any grass for the cattle. It just grows," referring to the natural ecology of the area's pampas.

As the waiter, smirking at Edelmar, unloaded marinated chunks of lamb onto our plates, I asked the rancher if he has to deal with a big water bill.

"You never have to water anything," he answered, his face glowing. "There is plenty of rain!" But being a farmer in Uruguay is not without its pitfalls. Edelmar imitated the contorted face his wife gives him when he returns from a soggy day in the field, his clothes smelling of livestock and fertile land.

Wildlife such as nutria and the endangered carpincho—the world's largest rodent—roam around at will on his ranch. "A baby carpincho comes by our house and we feed it milk. They're gentle things."

Carpincho are protected, but the wetlands-dotted Uruguayan state of Rocha, where his ranch is located, is known for its eager consumption of nutria, of which there is an overpopulation. I asked Edelmar if he partook in that particular bounty of his land. "If God put me on earth to raise cows and sheep," he said, pausing to chew, adding inadvertent drama to his statement, "then I'm going to eat cows and sheep."

He mentioned that several investors had approached him recently about renting out part of his land to well-heeled hunters. "I want to keep the land the way it is," he said, and then added, "why do something that doesn't make you happy?"

His revealing of his philosophy on money and its relationship to life led to a discussion of Argentineans—Uruguay's next door neighbors to the west and south—and how he views them as preoccupied with their image ("They think, 'Look at my car!'").

The skewered pork sausage accompanied his thoughts on the American economy. He revealed that he is a fan of Nelson DeMille thrillers as well as books analyzing American politics, perhaps the source of his fluent English. "Are you on the left or the right?" he asked me. I drew a circle in the air and said that the far left is indistinguishable from the far right, an answer that earned me a thumbs-up, his silverware stabbing the air in approval. By now, I realized that he wanted more than an English-language practice session. He wanted to discuss life philosophies and cultural matters with someone from afar. With someone from the land of Nelson DeMille.

When I was in the bathroom, he paid for my lunch, a maneuver that sent off a siren of suspicion; the what-does-he-really-want question throbbed in my head. In front of Edelmar, I hesitated. "If a friend came to your hometown of New York, you would show him around and buy him lunch, wouldn't you?" he asked.

I began to realize that his gesture was an extension of what I had already been experiencing south of the median, elsewhere in Uruguay: a proud chef in Montevideo inviting me behind the counter to check out his grilling technique, so close to the coals that I could feel the same heat he feels every day at work; storeowners uncorking histories of their family members who live in New Jersey and Michigan; a Brazilian couple, working inside a sausage cart in the capital, who, during a slow night, played me a round of melancholy chords on a guitar that had been handily stowed underneath the shelf of condiments.

Chuy—or Chuí—however it counts itself geographically, has been cultivating its own brand of amicability. Over the past century, doctors on the Brazilian side have tended to Uruguayan patients; the Uruguayan side ran electricity to the Brazilian side fifty years ago when the latter was still isolated from the rest of Brazil. The Brazilian side of the avenue, north of the median, is named Avenue Uruguay, while the Uruguayan side is named Avenue Brazil. As far as I know, Chuy is the only town in the world that holds a Carnival parade along an international border. It was as if the tandem towns themselves are two companions of mixed backgrounds who just like hanging out.

We walked to Edelmar's favorite duty-free shop, a concrete building with a spotless new façade on the other side of the avenue. After I bought a bottle of Uruguayan Tannat and he selected a plush Barney and a Spider-Man action figure, he mentioned that he would be taking the bus back to his ranch. Owning 4,000 head of cattle has not made him feel above utilizing Uruguay's convenient bus network.

We both discovered that we would be taking the same bus out of Chuy, headed west along the border. I would only be going a few kilometers outside of town, in search of a 280-year-old structure offering context to this border-straddling city: The Fort of San Miguel, a stone edifice that had passed between Portugal and Spain several times. I bid Edelmar goodbye and imagined the squeals of gratitude he'd hear when he arrived home.

The fort, on the Uruguayan side, had inspired the Portuguese name of the restaurant, La Fortaleza, at which I had just eaten. Such nomenclature would have been an unthinkable neighborly gesture in the days when Spain and Portugal bumped foreheads during their rabid land grabs in the New World. At that time, Amerindians still lived in the area, turning Europeans on to yerba mate tea. But the Amerindians didn't last long against gunpowder and syphilis.

Like any posturing European powers with God on their side and gold in their ballasts, the Portuguese and Spanish each needed fortifications. Big, imposing ones. Pity that the fort sits on the only hill in the area, making it a coveted parcel of wartime real estate. It is now a museum that overlooks kilometers of lagoons, wetlands, and pastures, with hundreds of snouts in the grass on both sides of the border. When I reached the clearing atop the hill, I was greeted by a hulking stone structure, silent and asleep, its slanted walls covered in orange lichen as if painted by a child.

I imagined how guards atop the walls would scan the horizon for signs of the other empire's troops amassing. I also wondered what they would have done if they knew that in two hundred years, not only would both empires be wiped off the continent, but a town like Chuy would be straddling the border, a town where people are allowed to come and go with as many forbidden alfajores or bottles of hot sauce as they wished. The fort, moat and all, seemed to serve as a monument to futility.

One of the fort's curators had apparently had the same idea because one of the cannons atop the rampart had been angled so that it would blast the adjacent corner of the fort if fired.

Walking over the drawbridge and into the courtyard, I found a room highlighting the sartorial trends of wartime past. That was where victims of war gave way to victims of fashion because one must indulge a peculiar vanity to enter battle in a tropical climate while wearing thick wool uniforms. The curator, whose voice I now imagined as being full of cackles and hoots, rounded up the most vibrant of these rugs-turned-jackets from the nineteenth century, fitted them on dummies, and stood them up next to one another, like a schoolteacher who had lined up troublemakers at the front of the classroom to embarrass them. I reached out and pinched one of the cuffs. The fabric was about the thickness of a deck of cards. I'd imagine any invaders stinking and melting inside those colorful button-ups would beg to get pushed into the nice, refreshing moat.

On another wall, the museum had stocked a glass case with officers' hats, boat-shaped and topped with fuzzy, mohawk-like protrusions. Perhaps their head plumage, especially the specimen that had been dyed a fashionable sky blue, represented some precursor to feathery drag queen attire for Carnival parades.

Funny how wars were waged back then, with bugle boys and female-repelling handlebar mustaches and an occasional surrender-over-a-cup-of-tea. But I did not want to get too cocky. Someone two hundred years from now might look at our present and snicker at America's scramble to control oil output that would run out in a few generations anyway. Such a future would render America's current involvement in the Middle East about as meaningful as a fort overlooking a border of tax-free Barney trafficking.

At the bottom of the hill, I waited across the Uruguayan customs office, a building with the size and informality of a gas station, for the next Chuy-bound bus. A few men seated in front seemed to be waiting for a bus, but they turned out to be customs officers. ALL VEHICLES MUST BE INSPECTED read the sign above the threshold. One of the officers would occasionally walk up to a driver-side window, appearing bothered that he had to get up at all, and ask a token question or two. The rest of the vehicles received nothing more than a few friendly waves from the crew. Inspection complete.

Back in town, amidst the neighborly chumminess, I hadn't yet found any of the recklessness associated with border locales. However, a restaurant on the Uruguayan side, which went by the catchy name Parrillada Jesus, offered a piece of promising hubris. Usually, the god-fearing Christians of Latin America attempt to push the buttons of various saints—the holy go-betweens—by naming streets, restaurants, plazas, and cities after them. But not in Chuy. They'd had it with that convoluted saintly overhead and decided to channel the Son of God directly. Eliminate the middleman! Just like the smugglers of Chuy's past had done.

I felt compelled to dine there. What other restaurant in town would dare serve better food than that of The Jesus Restaurant?

The kitchen was armed with a mainstay of Uruguayan pride: a six-foot, wood-fired parrillada, an impressive contraption that both sears and displays meat at the same time. But when I sat down, I knew something was wrong. Only a few other patrons dotted the dining room, hunched around bottles of beer and soda. The restaurant's parrillada was cold.

The waiter took the menu out of my hand and replaced it with a smaller munchies menu. Since they followed the standard Uruguayan dining schedule, their parrillada was dead from the early afternoon until 8 or 9 pm, something that both sides of the avenue must have known well. At that limbo hour—6 pm—the parrillada chef was long gone for the afternoon. I was only able to order an Uruguayan pizza, a thick, spongy piece of bread topped with half-melted cheese. Or was it an earthworm-covered dinner roll? Then again, Jesus was a carpenter, not a cook.

As much as I grumbled to myself about the limited windows of grill time, I thought of how the parrillada chef must be enjoying his afternoon off. Why work through the entire afternoon? I remembered Edelmar's words: "Why do something that doesn't make you happy?"

I found a seat on the bus that would return me to points further south in Uruguay. Before we left, a cop in a new, clean uniform stepped on. But she hadn't arrived to inspect duty-free maximums or even passport stamps, but to catch up with neighborhood friends, chuckling and ad-libbing, taking the ride home with everyone else.

Flip-flops with worn-through holes dangled into the aisle. Laps harbored crinkly bags stuffed with cigarette boxes and Brazilian jeans and Chivas Regal. I felt a brewing camaraderie with my fellow passengers because, along with them, I clutched my own duty-free wine and malagueta hot sauce, taking advantage of a place where the border doesn't divide countries, it joins them, as if to give the finger to the empires of the past.

I glanced out onto the motionless lagoons and the occasional fifty-year-old Ford carcass along the route, and I realized that the cultural vertigo had evaporated. Instead of considering each twist of language individually, instead of thinking of Chuy in terms of being part Uruguayan, part Brazilian, part duty free, or part anachronistic, I had realized that Chuy is its own animal, a species with a healthy appetite for quality of life and for whatever is grazing on Edelmar's ranch.

What the Walls Taught Me

We had climbed halfway up the staircase of a Valparaiso sidewalk when Salvador Dalí appeared. He was stenciled to the landing above, waiting for us with his perked-up handlebar mustache. For a closer look, my girlfriend Melanie and I stepped around another stray dog, his long body blocking almost the whole width of the concrete step. Valparaiso's take on multi-use public space.

Morning had barely arrived, and cargo ships at the port, in the distance below, had probably unloaded enough plastic silverware to outfit Chile's entire fast-food industry. Meanwhile, the hungover hills overlooking the port still slept, still hugged a blanket of overcast gauze. I wondered how many cans of Escudo beer the town had put back last night. And how many new stencils had been tattooed to its buildings?

Navigating the hillside topography of the city, we were hunting for said stencils and whatever layers of outdoor art we could discover. Decades of brush-stroke dialog—from political to phantasmal—have been blooming in a city that encourages murals as much as some other cities discourage them.

I felt oddly qualified for the undertaking. Thanks to having had just marked my thirty-eighth birthday, I had already been hosting a lively preoccupation with uncovering past layers of memories. I always find it remarkable how an arbitrary date such as a birthday has the power to unleash recollections, even when being 5,000 miles away from where I grew up in New England. Or perhaps it was not in spite of, but delivered by my Chilean surroundings: the wildly bright colors of the three-story houses stirring up the creations from marathon Lego-building sessions; or the city's steps I hopped up like bleachers during springtime high-school track practice.

At the same time, I was beginning to see that getting lost in an alien landscape—we had just arrived in Valparaiso a few days before—can often lead the traveler to learn as much about oneself as about the surroundings. The uncertainty and newness of travel tends to shake the mind out of a groove well-worn from repetition and comfort, melting off a congealed patina from atop one's thoughts and memories.

Unlike previous birthdays, however, the flashbacks didn't just show up and leave; they stung, vibrated, and loitered to remind me of time passing. I was beginning to heed age and its wholesale irreversibility.

I found that the city's murals offered a fortunate diversion from such matters. But I knew we would never find them all. Overlooking slanted steps as if to heckle pedestrians who slip on the abundance of dog turds, or hunkered down on trapezoidal spaces joining sidewalk and façade, the outdoor paintings of Valparaiso lie in wait, only revealing themselves footstep by footstep, wall by wall.

An exploratory, twenty-minute stroll managed to yield such preliminary prizes as a spray-painted Pope Benedict XVI picketing with a GOD NOT DEAD (sic) sign; abstract funiculars inspired by the city's creaky landmarks; stencils that refused to forget the abuse during Augusto Pinochet's 1973–1990 dictatorship, using a single red word PINOSHIT; giant eyes swimming in the confines of a threshold as if the door were a Steve Ditko comic book panel; and yet another stenciled rat parachuting in. It was at once dizzying and engrossing. I was eavesdropping on many silent conversations at the same time.

Like the strays blocking doorways, the murals and spray-can designs were mostly ignored by fanny-packed tourists who skipped past them. Perhaps the paintings, relatively young when compared to the age of the buildings, marred the image of what a city quarter bearing 125-year old UNESCO World Heritage townhouses was supposed to look like.

But I found it difficult to separate the houses, hanging barnacle-like atop cliffs, from the artwork that accompanied them on the street. I noticed that as the rusted roofs and chipped trim spoke of a port that had seen more lucrative days decades ago, the paintings on the walls both announced the residents' current visions while also recalling the elder city's architecture and transportation methods, each era giving the other context.

What I soon realized about this street-level communication was what remained nearly absent: billboards and other advertisements. Before us, every inch of paint and dye—of

both the houses' riotously bright colors and the artwork—
had been applied by hand. That could have been why even
though few people walked around the hills in the morning,
the streets felt human.

To an American like me who has had glossy, corporate-
conglomerate ads railroaded into him since his youth
(damn that Bubblicious jingle), I have expected that high-
visibility walls become call girls for the highest bidder.
Shouldn't the landing of that staircase drip with mantras
about the latest sneakers, and how trendy and fulfilled
you'll feel when wearing them?

Instead, Valparaiso puts forth a much more even playing
field of communication. The speculator's battle cry of
"whatever the market will bear" seems silenced when it
comes to how a Valparaiso wall should be adorned. VAL-
PARAISO IS NOT FOR SALE, shouted a stenciled hit on a zinc-
walled house we had just passed. England-based graffiti artist Banksy justifies his public art as a counterpoint to paid
advertisements that one is forced to look at every day. As
we climbed and descended the hills of the city, we noticed
his multi-colored stencil style influencing the high-contrast
Natalie-Portmans-with-sniper-rifles and the dancing Elvises
hanging out on staircases.

Not that equality comes without its problems. The same
fairness that allows anyone with presumed permission
from a house's owner to paint a mural is the same fairness
that encourages anyone with a spray can to use the walls as
a message board. Scrawled mantras—leftist, rightist, pro-
homosexual, anti-yuppie—seem to breed overnight. The
line between what is of cultural value and what is vandalism will always remain subjective, but judging from the unmistakable lushness of the city's outdoor art, Chile deems

the freedom worth the trouble it brings, since Chileans dealt with enough graffiti police under Pinochet.

In a way, however, the system tends to govern itself. Instances of narcissistic, tag-style graffiti—glorified names free of any purpose other than declaring "so-and-so wuz here"—rarely gain respect outside of the tagger and his few buddies, rarely last without being painted over, and rarely make it into photo books sold in the city's art boutiques, as is the case with many of the more beloved stencils and murals. It's an odd place for street art—the photo books both validating the art and stripping it of its environment—yet above all, the books reflect the reality that street art has become part of the fabric of the city.

I can easily understand such support for street art in a country that, in 2008, awarded government grants to jazz bands and indie comic book artists. Imagine one's tax dollars funding a comic book featuring a character called *Super Vaca*, or Super Cow, who drives a garbage truck and battles a foe who looks suspiciously like Pinochet, and you'd be imagining what it means to be Chilean.

Art historian Rod Palmer, in his book *Street Art Chile*, found that the roots of the tradition dig down to former president Salvador Allende, who utilized political murals that started a street art war with his opponent in the 1963 elections. (Allende is still celebrated in Valparaiso by his stenciled likeness.) When Pinochet seized control, his goons painted over the murals, both political and otherwise. In 1991, after his exit, street art began to reappear. As if to make up for lost time, two local painters teamed up with Valparaiso's Catholic University to select a score of well-known artists, several of which had just returned from exile, to hit the retaining walls and houses of Bellavista Hill, a central knuckle poking from the city's undulating landscape. Their pieces belong to what is known as the *Museo a Cielo Abierto*, or the Open Sky Museum.

Balancing ourselves on smooth cobblestones, our shoes groping for level ground, Melanie and I entered a web of streets doubling as the Museo itself. Some of the artists, whose works hang in indoor galleries, preferred the indoor mindset and painted perfectly rectangular pieces in the centers of irregular, terrain-dependent surfaces. Perhaps their message was to expand the idea of where traditional art can appear.

Meanwhile, the others worked the awkward shapes and bends into their designs, using the terrain as an inspiration rather than a limitation, the city itself becoming an artistic influence. Outside the streets of the museum, muralists used similar approaches. Images swallowed and digested drainpipes and doorways. One patch of sidewalk steps bordered a polygonal canvass framing ant-like cats dining on cigarettes, leading me to wonder what Dalí, whose mug appeared again down the street, would have thought of this offspring of his surrealism. Ghostly fatsos floated next to thresholds—telltale works of an itinerant Canadian artist known as Hecho, whose characters often appear in collages with local artists, such collaborations furthering Chile's artistic cross-pollination.

On an inclined façade, we encountered a black and white mural spanning a doorway that I later recognized as the work of Fran & Frisura, a college-age duo to whom Palmer devoted several pages, owing to their distinctive use of figures combining facial features of pre-Columbian art with robotic brains and innards. It was as if they were hacking time itself, warping the past with the future. In this particular piece, the duo responded to the irregular shape of the surface by painting a squat figure (a chessboard's knight) on the shorter side of the space and a thinner character (a rook) on the taller end. Each of their murals could never exist anywhere else, even on another wall around the corner, without changing in some way.

I imagined what might happen if a mural had somehow been carefully removed from its perch on the street and hung in a museum. As you walk past the humorless museum guard, you place your hands behind your back and give a slight, obligatory nod while examining a flat, framed piece titled something like STREET ART STUDY, without its context of brick textures and shapes, without a faded Volkswagen carcass convalescing in front of it, without seagulls squawking overhead, without a dog turd slalom at your feet, and without the piston-pumping of your lungs from climbing twelve stories of sidewalk stairs to reach the piece.

There is an obvious advantage, however, to scoring an installation in an indoor gallery: longevity. On the street, free of enclosures that preserve the vibrancy of the paint, the murals lie exposed to the thirsty bleaching of the sun. And no security guards (humorless or otherwise) protect the murals from the whims of spray cans. A pungent example: when we neared the location of Museo's mural #3, painted by Eduardo Pérez (dean of the school of visual arts at Santiago's Universidad Mayor), we first encountered a trio of high school–aged art students, crouched on a staircase landing, sketching the poetic geometry of the hills onto oversized pads propped up on their knees. When we discovered that a graffiti tag had recently destroyed Pérez's mural that had been painted onto a surface a few steps from the students, the sound of pencils shuffling across paper stopped.

I turned to find their eyes on us. The one closest to us tucked his chin-length mop of hair behind his ear and said softly, "It was a beautiful work," as if he felt obliged to apologize for the behavior of one of his countrymen.

However, nineteen remaining open-air museum pieces are nineteen more than were up under Pinochet, a dictator America helped to install in power. Maybe I should have been the one apologizing for some of my countrymen. With arcing gestures of pencils, the students guided us to some of the Museo's other pieces nearby. The swishing percussion of sketching resumed.

Later, on an adjacent hill, I found myself staring at a mural of trompe-l'œil paper airplanes—complete with a hand throwing one of them—as I realized that two functioning windows, probably leading into someone's living room, were at the center of the piece. Did the art become part of the wall, or did the wall become part of the art?

IN THE CATACOMBS of a Valparaiso cathedral, Super Vaca had just walked into a trap. He realized his misfortune when he encountered the remains of a mad doctor, a gurgling head in a bell jar, who asked to be turned to get a better view of the impending action. Too bad for Doc—no one paid attention to him and he missed the spectacle of his boss, the Supreme Commander, gobbling a pill that turned himself into an octopus with a head resembling a particular dictator from Chile's recent past. With one of his tentacles, the Commander greedily seized Super Vaca and swung him around the cathedral. *¡Blamm! ¡Cromm! ¡Clanck!* How will our hero escape from the suckers of a dictatorial cephalopod?

Chile's peculiar stick-thin geography, racking up 4,000 miles of coastline rich in marine life, had fortified our hero with the experiences necessary to neutralize the threat. In the next panel, Super Vaca, like any self-respecting Chilean confronted with fresh seafood, took a bite out of the tentacle.

I'd decided to allow whatever apparent mid-life (two-fifths life?) crisis that was fermenting inside me to tire itself out, and that was when I finished reading Valparaiso artist Renzo Soto's *Super Vaca: Historias Negras* on my birthday, finding a comic book perfect for channeling the past via the energy of escapist youth. After I had navigated the painted fantasy worlds on the walls of the city for the past several days, the story of a hero with horns of a bull and a talent for defending himself with his appetite appeared a little less impossible.

MOST OF THE STRAYS we encountered were either chewing on garbage or sitting on the streets like kings on thrones, taking visceral joy in forcing us bipeds to walk around them. But one moist-smelling specimen decided to follow us until it hopped ahead and began leading us up a staircase to a tight passageway awash in a crowded, boisterous congregation of murals. Even the staircase itself bore a painting of funiculars climbing and descending on the fronts of its steps, viewable only from the bottom landing, a reward for the skill of both artist and viewer. I tingled with satisfaction. We had found what seemed like a secret little pocket of the city.

With scratchy puffs of dog breath, the pug led us to a figure hunkered down near a hostel entrance, the young man's curled frame leaning into a shoebox-sized Model-A roadster he was painting onto a stoop. He moved his brush in a slow, delicate stroke, as if to charm the image out of his mind and onto the concrete. At last, we caught one of the city's elusive vandals in the act!

Like a host greeting guests in his living room, our criminal, his soft skin clinging to sharp cheekbones, offered us a gentle smile, the kind where the eyes smile too. He scratched the dog's neck as he bent away from his creation to let us inspect his progress. His busy fingers kept releasing more of the ripeness of the pug, apparently not a stray after all. I complimented him on his dreamy take on a metallic subject and added, "Your dog brought us here."

He answered, "He's the hostel's house pet." The artist barely filled out his smock embroidered with the words HOSTAL BELLAVISTA; I found the same name spelled out in a tile mosaic under him. He told us that the Model-A was his latest offering to the hostel, as he had already completed several of the designs surrounding us on the passageway. Making beds, painting streets, cuddling pets—all in a day's work in the Valparaiso hospitality industry.

THE AFTERNOON CLOUDS burned up, allowing the sun's rays to poke and finger the alleyways. Melanie and I leaned on a railing, staring down a crevice of a street where a slice of the port came into view. Her gentile insistence on taking a break had reminded me just how obsessive my mural hunting had become. Track practice was finally over. And thanks to our stillness, I began to view the hillsides as would the art students with sketchpads on their laps.

I could not deny the tug the city had on me. But I knew that not everyone could care for a place where, at that moment, somewhere else in the city, someone had taken a shortcut down the wrong pedestrian stairway and was being mugged. Somewhere on a metal rooftop, a stray dog was caught up in an indulgent snooze, stretched out impressively thin like spilled cake batter. Somewhere, an art student waited until a street was deserted and pulled out a cardboard stencil hidden inside her sketchpad.

The sunshine revealed the seams of the city's layered eras—brick, corrugated zinc, rust, paint, retaining walls, more paint. The port was carrying its years proudly, especially considering that there are many ways a city can age. A city could simply decay into nothingness from neglect. Or it may be perpetually groomed in the same style in an attempt to keep its appearance static, becoming its own travel advertisement that never needs updating, the Botox of urban preservation. Or it could be constantly converted into whatever scene the current wave of capital demands, a city that has no past. And then there's Valparaiso, with its slowly settling foundations; its encroachment of feral fur in equilibrium with its rent-paying residents, keeping human development in an earthly perspective; its artwork that has been refreshing the city without replacing it, cultivating a traversable funicular of continuity that creates an intoxicating cocktail of eras and desires and dimensions. As I age, I hope to age like Valparaiso.

Off the Clock in the Colchagua Valley

Nothing says "wine is our religion" more than a twenty-foot-high cross built out of barrels.

Melanie and I had just passed the roadside cross as we entered Santa Cruz, a town in Chile's Colchagua Valley—a region in the center of a fertile trough that runs over 1,000 miles down the length of the country's narrow profile. On any other day, it might have been an ideal place to investigate the area's work ethic that has, in just two decades, catapulted the international image of Chile's wine from jug-bound mediocrity to cork-dork collectability. But we arrived when the Colchagua Valley was about to hold its yearly grape harvest festival in Santa Cruz. An investigation into the valley's play ethic would have to suffice.

I looked forward to a celebration of the region's economic livelihood, with copious amounts of said economic livelihood pumping around revelers' numbed limbs. Even better, this year's celebration promised to hold an unpredictable swelling of passion, thanks to a challenge of a neighborhood smackdown. When funds to hold the festival in its traditional setting—Santa Cruz's central plaza—had been withdrawn owing to a political rivalry, the organizers moved the festival to another town, San Fernando, twenty-five miles away. But the valley must really like to party because both towns planned to hold their own competing festivals, dueling with corkscrews, doubling the debauchery. Saint versus saint. And who knows, I thought, I might need to duck under volleys of slurred insults shooting across the valley.

Sure, the central plaza in Santa Cruz presented us with a park full of stands from local wineries, for which we bought our tasting tickets. But as we would notice right away, the festival was not about wine alone. Understanding that wine is a natural and expected partner of food, the town had bolstered its bottled arsenal with a bulwark of barbecue pits whose swirly tentacles of grill smoke we had smelled five blocks away. Split pig carcasses hung near fire pits, vanquished, crucified, displayed. At ground zero, the smoke swarming about the square teased and stung our faces and blocked our vision. A fog of meat.

A sea of t-shirt-wearing city folk, many from nearby Santiago, marched around the park, not looking where they were going, clumsily bumping their way past others (tearing away wine's supposedly elitist mystique). Wallets trustingly in back pockets, flip-flops slapping pasty heels. It was full-on party time in *el campo*. To my disappointment, I could not find any posters declaring "the original harvest festival is here" or "the other saint drinks vinegar."

We did, however, find a schedule, posted in the center of the square, that listed hourly traditional dancing performances and even activities to show off the festival's beauty queen contestants. I wondered if the organizers would follow the schedule in such intense party-time conditions. A more festive question I pondered, though, was what a beauty pageant had to do with wine. The answer was on the schedule. At eight o'clock, the pageant's contestants would take off their princess pumps and trample grapes on the main stage.

While walking around the perimeter of the park, Melanie and I passed a procession of the nine pageant contestants, all dressed in matching white dresses, each wearing a sash inscribed with the name of a grape, salon hair tumbling elegantly onto bare shoulders. None of them was a day over twenty. They instinctively wore wholesome smiles as we passed, perhaps a gesture to score last-minute votes because along with our drink tickets we were each given a ballot.

The grape stomp, I imagined, would be an effective way for a contestant to break away from the pack of pretty faces. Technique and style points and all. But eight o'clock arrived and went, and the stage remained alight with dancers spinning their bright bolero jacket costumes to the fiery acoustic guitar strums of the Spanish- and Andean-inspired *cueca*, as they had been doing for hours. It seemed the Chileans had said the hell with the schedule; they just wanted to have fun. The lack of public clocks echoed this sentiment. I asked a pot-bellied spectator with his daughter on his shoulders if he knew when the beauty queens and grapes would meet. I was met with an unhurried grin and a whole-body nod. *"No sé."* (I don't know.)

We filled up our glasses with a berry-like Carménère and found a clear view of the stage. As much as I felt clever for predicting the downfall of the schedule, I found myself at a loss when considering the cueca, Chile's national dance that shares its name with its music. Chilean folklore tells us that the dance mimics a rooster courting a hen, each dancer circling the other in half-moon sequences. But the white handkerchiefs that each twirled overhead looked less like flying poultry feathers and more like instruments with which a dancer would lash the other if one spotted a weakness. The fast-footed men in black riding boots with spurs, along with the women wearing long, ruffled dresses and smiles too wide and too indulgent for simple theatrical effect, made it clear that any pending attack wasn't going to happen. And the cueca spun and spun, maintaining a playful tension.

Each 6/8-time cueca song worked the same major chords and the same tempo, save a different troupe of dancers. I yearned for a minor chord or two, just for a moment, just to break things up. No one else seemed to need such variety. Santa Cruz kept the cueca churning, hour after hour. It seemed as if the whole town—and the visitors— were waiting around for their turn to put on a costume and dance on stage.

There was something about the Chilean's passion for cueca I found fascinating. In travel, when I experience the sights and sounds and scents of a different culture, I sometimes feel a sort of dislocation, one that is not necessarily uncomfortable, but instead excitingly tangible. I feel out of sync, humbled, sensing an unquantifiable depth of the place.

As intoxicating as the feeling may have been, the desire to understand my surroundings soon took over. However, I was discovering that it would take more than knowledge of grape varietals and fermentation tanks to gain an understanding of this valley's celebration of wine. I glanced at a family of four standing in front of us, stretching their necks toward the stage like poppies toward the sun. They only broke posture to chew on *choripans*, pork sausage sandwiches. Taking a cue from the family, a choripan was in order to key me in to the day's rhythm of meat and dance. The choripan didn't require sauce because the bun diligently captured the sausage drippings while the Carménère acted as a slick, fruit-filled liaison.

Melanie and I traded drink tickets for glasses of velvety Cabernet. We barely comprehended the S-dropped Spanish of the young, overwhelmed woman at the stand (*"do' boleto"*—two tickets, I thought she barked), adding a linguistic layer to our dislocation. In lieu of a grape stomp, we wandered the side streets around the square. We gnawed on slabs of lean wild boar fresh off the grill and navigated around assorted party spillage—a peanut vendor staring into space near his hand-painted cart, young lovers sharing ice cream in a faded threshold, an obstacle course of wobbly drunkenness. Between two parked cars stood a musical family consisting of Mom turning the music box crank, Junior hopping around in a strapped-on percussion suit (with a bright Chilean flag on the drum head), and Dad managing the whole act by leaning on a car and watching. I should note that none of the festivities involved lectures on the agricultural benefits of diurnal temperature variation or lessons on how to swirl wine in a glass.

When we returned to the square, I wondered if we had wandered long enough for Santa Cruz to fire up some grape mashing. We squeezed into the melee of clutched wine glasses and slowly spun around. The choripan was still grilling, the dancers still stalking, the hankies still spinning. Doubtful of any eminent reappearance of beauty queens, we left the square.

As we stepped away, I took a few pictures of the square's squat colonial buildings against a rich purple launch of nightfall, one that seemed to arrive late, as if the Chilean sky also held a disregard for schedules. We were not the only ones who had noticed the scene; we found a man from Santiago, in sandals and khaki shorts, kneeling and photographing the same buildings. I asked him what he thought of the wine tonight. "The wine was not very good," he said in a flat, sour air. Then he added, "The bigger wineries are at San Fernando." Melanie and I weren't feeling the same pessimism about Santa Cruz's tipples. But in the interest of full knowledge, San Fernando would be our next stop.

RARELY DOES SOMEONE score a second chance to attend a once-per-year event in the same year. But the next day, thanks to Colchagua Valley politics, Melanie and I took a taxi across the valley to San Fernando to assess the challenging town's party time worthiness. We came prepared to accept fresh sorties of Syrah, Cabernet, Carménère, and choripans.

Our first mistake was turning up on time. When will we learn? None of the wine stalls were pouring yet. Most of the wineries had not even arrived. Not to be outdone by its sister town, however, the grillers of San Fernando were already basting spit-impaled meat with fat brushes suitable for painting a barn. They were positioning the spits over barbecue pits so large they must have been visible in satellite photos.

Like its cross-valley rival, San Fernando used the festival as an excuse to celebrate everything about the valley, whether it involved wine or not. Melanie and I were the first customers at the stall selling locally made vanilla-scented soap and at another selling broccoli-flavored bonbons. We were the first to hear the business-like sales pitch from the horse jerky vendor, a thin, tiny woman with an incongruously loud voice. We would hear the same serious delivery every time we passed her stall: "Made from only the best cuts of meat. Low in saturated fat!" From that point on, whenever I spotted a horse grazing in a field in Chile, I grappled with an uneasy urge to say to him, "Don't break your leg."

Since my warning was too late for the fellow that ended up in the vacuum-sealed bags on display, I bought one, hoping that, as with choripan, eating horse jerky would help ease me into more of a Chilean frame of mind. After all, the nearby Andes, overlooking us from the east, were the birthplace of the dried, salted meat known in Quechua as *ch'arki*, the word that gives us the English word jerky. But soon the horse's revenge arrived in the form of the jerky itself, which resembled clippings of a shag rug that had been left on a barn floor. As if to say, "Try pairing *that* with wine, sucker."

At least I could look forward to another shot at capturing the spectacle of beauty queens in a pool of grapes, I thought. We waited while cueca dancers and their hand-kerchief propellers dominated the stage. Foot traffic in the square had succumbed to a thick, impassable gel of love handles and the sweaty t-shirts that attempted to cover them. Several skewers, choripans, and redeemed wine tickets later, we realized that an all-too-familiar zeal for cueca was playing itself out with no regard for the activity-packed schedule. On that level, San Fernando was keeping up rather well with the other town down the road. But, despite warnings from the khaki-clad urbanite from the day before, we found the reds and whites of both festivals just as amiable to a choripan.

Just like thc elusive girl-on-grape action, the cross-valley battle I had anticipated never materialized. And no one seemed to have an anxious, groupie-like obsession in anticipation of the queens. Not that the square was without its fixations—people lined up to get their picture taken in front of the barbecuing pig carcasses. At a Chilean festival, the meat is a celebrity.

And that was as close as we came to the groupie-swarmed celebrities of the Colchagua Valley.

The next day, Melanie and I decided to visit a few wineries before heading to the train station. Our innkeeper was perplexed by our insistence on rushing, and that was when he dropped a painful little fact on us: Chile had observed daylight saving time two days before, turning the clocks back one hour. (Since I would hate to feel like the only dope, I will mention that Copa Airlines also adjusted their flights by an hour and never bothered telling any of their customers.) Chile wasn't late. We were early.

Not even a mouthful of horse jerky was able to guide my awareness toward such a mundane but significant reality as the correct local hour. Such a temporal mismatch proved to be an apt metaphor for this traveler's cultural dislocation.

I asked our innkeeper about the beauty contestants. Yes, the town did indeed crown a queen (Señorita Carménère). For all I knew, when we abandoned the respective festival squares in impatient haste, the beauty contestants from Santa Cruz could have been wrestling the contestants from San Fernando in a vat of grapes, with the resulting wine to be sold to the highest bidding pervert.

Chowhounding Peru, from Anticuchos to Zaino

Peruvian friend of mine living in the States once squarely told me, "Peru is not known for its cuisine."

Perhaps he held such a conviction because the mountaintop ruins of Machu Picchu dazzle most of Peru's visitors and overshadow all else, relegating food and drink to the duty of humble hiking fuel, except for a pisco sour or two.

Or was my friend playfully trying to provoke my curiosity? Melanie and I had decided to begin our quest for answers at his old stomping grounds of Pucallpa, an urban enclave in the middle of Peru's lowland rainforest. With its zinc-roofed stalls and windshield-free, three-wheeled taxis launching red dust into the viscous tropical heat, the often forgotten Pucallpa seems not the quaintest corner of Peru, a fact that keeps Pucallpa off the trodden tourist trail.

My hotel even assumed that, as a foreign visitor, I must have worked in either the lumber trade or the agriculture business, two of the main industries of the area. Being neither, I discovered quickly that Pucallpa's location on the Ucayali River, an Amazonian tributary, blesses the working class city with a tantalizing bounty of provisions from the surrounding jungle.

Its residents have long since learned to make a rewarding dinner out of *zaino* (collared peccary), its incomparable succulence drubbing its domesticated, floppy-eared porcine counterpart. Or the petite South American deer. Or a juicy, flame-grilled steak of *majás*, a large jungle rodent. Majás may not acquire fans among the gastronomically conservative, and that's unfortunate since the flavorful tropical meat makes a shell steak look like a timid understudy.

We tried all three for 19 soles ($6) at a local restaurant across from the Ruiz Hotel while a swarm of hand-painted *motokars* (three-wheeled taxis) whined past the open windows, seasoning our plates with just a hint of red dirt and blue smoke. If I didn't speak Spanish, I could have always ordered lunch by pointing to the stuffed majás atop the shelf in the restaurant's dining room.

To counter the thick broth better known as the air of the lowland interior, sidewalk kiosks sell cups of *chicha morada*, a sweet, non-alcoholic drink of purple corn, sugar, and cinnamon. Every time we asked for the drink *para llevar* (for takeaway), the vendor ladled it into the standard Peruvian to-go container: a plastic bag with a straw in it.

Holding one of the sloshing half-sol (15¢) prizes reminded me of winning a bagged goldfish at a carnival, except that I had to figure out how to drink it. For one-handed operation, the trick is to grip the bag at the top loosely enough to allow the juice to run up the straw, but firmly enough to avoid dropping it.

Some Amazonian beverages offer benefits above thirst placation. When I ordered a shake of the pulpy *aguaje* fruit at an open-air restaurant next to the city square, the young waitress froze her face into a twist of perplexed suspicion. Later that day, I found out why. After a forty-five-minute taxi ride up a dirt road, we met a community of indigenous Shipibo at the town of San Francisco, where the villagers had just returned from harvesting a basket of—coincidentally—aguaje.

Despite decades of being marginalized by the encroachment of industry that polluted nearby Lake Yarinaqucha, the village still retains much of its knowledge of the jungle. "Aguaje is very healthy," one of the Shipibo women stated, pointing at the bumpy red fruit.

I was just about to add—smugly—that I had enjoyed a glass of it for lunch when she continued with, "It is loaded with hormones beneficial to women." I didn't end up growing breasts, but I furtively began selecting other fruits for subsequent beverages.

Grapes grow surprisingly well where the jungle meets the Andean mountain slopes far northwest of the city. But I didn't expect *Wine Spectator* to dispatch its best team of slurp-and-spit reviewers, armed with DEET and thesauri, into the malarial wilderness. Instead of focusing on wine-making, the growers of the Amazon region more commonly spike the juice with *aguardiente*, or cane liquor, forming the unruly drink *uvachado*.

It pairs well with long waits for late-arriving planes at the Pucallpa airport while one enjoys the tarmac's view of grime-shrouded helicopter carcasses from past military days. Uvachado is so far from wine that the makers drop a few fresh grapes into each plastic bottle so the drinker won't forget what it is made from.

YOU MIGHT THINK that a cow's heart, thumping a half billion beats in a lifetime, would end up suitable for nothing more than leathering a saddle. But after Peruvian cooks marinate and season strips of the cow heart with cumin and achiote, the strips become tender *anticuchos*, the popular skewered street treat we enjoyed from food carts on the sidewalks of Pucallpa as well as the more familiar destinations of Lima and Cuzco.

And speaking of more familiar destinations, we traveled to Cuzco, in the Andean highlands, to search for one of Peru's historically popular dishes—*cuy*, or guinea pig. Archaeological evidence indicates that guinea pigs have been domesticated in Peru since 2,500 B.C. The country's penchant for cuy continues unhindered. Peruvians devour 65 million of the rodents per year, and to satisfy the demand, a Peruvian university has recently bred a guinea pig that reaches twice the normal size.

Peruvians from all over the country enjoy cuy, but I singled out Cuzco because a local artist who painted a mural for the city's cathedral reimagined *The Last Supper* by depicting a guinea pig on a plate in front of Jesus. After an afternoon of scaling the city's stone stairways while sucking in the impenitently thin air of 10,900 feet (3,322 m) above sea level, we were ready for some cuy as well.

While Jesus and his twelve disciples had to share a lone, scrawny, 1½-pound (¾-kg) animal, I ordered my very own. I first sampled cuy at the elegant Inca Grill, where the cuy arrived already cut up and glazed in a yellow pepper and rosemary sauce.

The local cafés on the outskirts of the city, however, cook up a more traditional and less expensive cuy, its head and claws frozen in a roasted crispness. If you like rabbit, you'll like cuy. Pet or protein? The answer seems to depend on one's cultural perspective.

For afternoon libations in the highlands, buckets of pasty froth sit at street corners, ready for action. I'm talking about *chicha*. Fortunately, the home brews, made from fermented grains or fruits and sold for a half sol per glass, taste better than they look.

The strawberry chicha from the outdoor produce market in Ollantaytambo reminded me of fruity Belgian beers. It made for a soothing choice of beverage while we gazed at the mountainside Incan ruins that towered over the town like golems paused in mid-romp. "Another?" asked the chicha vendor as she cleaned the glasses on her apron.

When exploring side streets of the southern city of Puno, I joined the patient bustle surrounding the warmth of refrigerator-sized stalls hawking servings of *salchipapa*— a contraction of *salchicha* (sausage) and *papa* (potato)—for under a dollar. The cheap eats would have been a rather pedestrian pile of French fries and cut-up hot dogs if not for the mellow hit of the *salsa de aceituna* (olive sauce) squirted on top. Puno's decadently thick salsa de aceituna ruined me for ketchup.

As with most travelers to Puno, we took a boat from its port to the fragile islands inside Lake Titicaca, sloshing around at a crisp 12,725 feet (3,879 m) above sea level. Our ultimate destination was the island of Amantani, a cold, dusty cone of dirt hulking up from the center of the lake.

Just what could be for dinner on this apparently desolate isle? Upon arrival, the island's geography gave us the hairy eyeball, but in defiance, the families hosting guests stewed together what little grows on the island and served us savory soups of quinoa and several varieties of potato, some creamy, some crumbly, others with tangy skin. The meals, finished with fried cheese, were simple but energizing.

Many of the island's adobe-brick houses are caressed by the vines of the tangy citrus fruit *granadilla*, a few of which Martinez, the father of our host family, plucked off for us. "After you plant them, they just grow on their own," he told us of the robust vine, providing us with an appropriate metaphor for what may be the islanders' own survival philosophy.

Clothing fashioned from alpaca wool abounds in the Andean highlands, and so do opportunities to enjoy alpaca steak. Alpaca is a shorter cousin of the llama, both of which have been bred by Andean cultures for thousands of years, the former for its wool and meat, and the latter for its strength.

Alpaca can bring in more money for the herder if the animal is sheared every two years for its wool instead of being turned over to the sauté pan, so there is a higher cost for its entry on a menu, usually $9 or more. Back in Cuzco, I interpreted its cleanly rich flavor as what would happen if a pig were crossed with a lamb (no word on what the animals would think of that date). Mint jelly not required.

From sit-down restaurants to sidewalk stalls, Peruvian cuisine seems to be a jealously protected secret, minus the jealousy and protection. Flame-grilled majás may be far from worldwide fame, but I'd still like to add to my friend's original statement: Peru is not known for its cuisine—yet.

The Peanut Fiends of Guayaquil

Downtown Guayaquil is a formidable example of urban hegemony. It is carpeted over with concrete, car honks have ousted bird songs, and the bordering Guayas River is an opaque procession of death and stink. Architects of the new boardwalk have recalled the site's jungle days with a few manicured garden strips, but nearby, the builders lessened the effect by installing a bunch of welded, airport-generic doohickeys in a McDonaldland color scheme. Just one more ton of cinder blocks and the city might have nature bound and gagged.

So that, at least, was the first impression the city slid my way when I arrived in a taxi squeaking out the requisite honking before every intersection (horns keep traffic moving better than watching mute stoplights, apparently). Here, the vibrancy of tropical lushness has given way to a different kind of life, Guayaquil's unstoppable street bustle: scooters carrying two or more people, trick ice cream that never melts, nipple-studded tabloids, violent cracks of sugar cane juicers. I stepped over cords of handsets—dragged outside storefronts and placed on stools—which served as improvised pay phones. I dodged the soda men, each with a two-liter bottle in one hand and plastic cups in the other. For a quarter, they'll pour you a serving to combat the sticky sunshine. Fanta is a welcome friend when tree shade is wanting.

The city's downplaying of the environment seemed all the more punctuated when I remembered that Guayaquil is the birthplace of Mike Judge, whose animated delinquents Beavis and Butthead routinely use frogs as baseballs and throw dogs and cats into washing machines.

But as I would discover, not all critters have succumbed to a sarcophagus of heat-preserving concrete (or to the hands of off-duty Burger World employees). I'm talking about two hundred frolicking iguanas that sized me up and surrounded me when I stepped into the city's pint-sized Parque Bolivar, or Bolivar Park.

From the street, the block appeared as another standard park featuring another standard statue of the hero of northern South American liberation, Simon Bolivar. But make no mistake—it's clear who rules this rare enclave of foliage. As I felt my shirt gripping the sweat on my back, a chunky scent, like that of a lair, weighed down the shade under the park's fifty-foot trees and refused to be carried away by the breeze. I entered with care because so many iguanas were selfishly sunning themselves on the crosswalks, leaving a slalom course of three-foot tails to navigate. Was this one of the biblical plagues that the scribes had accidentally omitted? Perhaps an early rough draft of the scriptures included the passage "And then God sent the nonbelievers legions of ugly dragons whose hunger could not be quelled..." Or something like that.

Then I looked up. For every iguana in front of me on the path, I was able to spy another two or three holding court in the branches above, and another few noisily clawing their way up or down the tree trunks.

It didn't matter how many gawking people were in the park. There were always more iguanas than people. And who is gawking at whom? And who is truly fenced in? While a low gate kept humans from entering the grassy patches, the iguanas stomped their claws wherever they pleased—on the stone paths, through the fence holes, on the grass, in burrows, up in the trees, all over the heads of statues. Yes, that's right: It doesn't matter if you're the mother of Jesus. The iguanas will still camp out on the forehead of your chiseled likeness, and give you that king-of-the-hill taunt. The sight provided me with a sampling of what will happen if humans suddenly vanish from the earth. Our architecture would become the jungle gym of all the world's critters. It would be permanent recess.

As thick reptile musk crawled into my lungs, I imagined what it must be like to cling about in the iguanas' airy perches high up in the canopies. From their vantage point, the flat walking paths at ground level must look like an ant farm for lumbering bipeds. Any human far below could serve as your makeshift toilet.

How could urbanization have failed to squeeze out the park's little squatters? Guayaquileños, or folks from Guayaquil, don't always agree. They have two theories. Either the iguanas were always in the area and became confined to the park as development incrementally muscled in, or the block became an unwanted pet repository—kind of like Manhattan's Central Park—and the dynamics of feral lust took over. And then there's the biblical plague theory that I just made up.

In any case, these iguanas have no predators. Despite being on Latin America's menu for centuries (in Latin America, iguanas are referred to as *pollo de palo*, or "chicken of the tree"), it is forbidden to hunt the lucky herps in Parque Bolivar. Chalk up one more liberation for Simon B.

In fact, their only means of population control seems to be curiosity. When the guard wasn't busy fishing turtles out of the park's pond with a pool skimmer for lucrative photo-ops, he mentioned to me that iguanas occasionally feel the desire to explore outside their park and wander out into the street. Sadly, that's where the tires of Russian-made Ladas serving as the city's cabs promptly cut the iguanas' vacations short. *Pollo de calle* (chicken of the street), an opportunistic Guayaquileño might say.

For the ones that stay in the park, it's all about free lunch. Every noon, park guards toss in a few buckets of cucumbers or lettuce cores to supplement the iguana's leaf-devouring diet. Other than that, though, the iguanas take care of themselves, breeding at will (your branch or mine?), snorting in polluted air, their drilling eyes—especially right before a fight—similar to those on a crowded subway car.

I even happened upon the beginnings of a three-way fight right on the heat of the slate walkway. By that time, the lair-like odor acted as reptilian Ritalin, helping me notice that the three huddled iguana noses lay poised and motionless at perfect 120-degree angles from one another. I even blocked out the nonstop beep-beeping of stuttering Lada horns as I studied the conflict.

But such beautiful symmetry began to degrade into displays of slimy tongues and ominous head-bobs. Without a sound, the gathering burst into a twirling brown ball—like fruit on a slot machine—but ended in a stalemate for all three participants. They just split up and resumed sunning themselves, as if they had changed their minds about the whole pecking order thing.

After all, they had much more enjoyable things to do. Like scaring children. It's as if the Ecuadorian parents are in cahoots with the iguanas because the parents keep egging on their kids to grab the creatures' tails, while all but the bravest kids form peanut-shaped horror mouths and nod sideways and whine.

Speaking of peanuts, a bag of them will bring out one of the iguana's more memorable urban adaptations. Sure, their skin has already turned from the fresh green of a wet-behind-the-dewlap jungle iguana to a hipster brown—to match the pollution, of course. But anyone who sits on a bench and opens up a bag of peanuts will be accosted by a bunch of hungry lizards that will beg like dogs. (Give them a few more generations and they'll probably start wagging their tails too.) Naturally, the kids get it the worst. I think I'll always associate Guayaquil with a pack of mini-dinosaurs pawing at a child's thigh, begging for a handout, all while the kids are wailing, their trembling extremities pulled in and away from thrusting, scaly cheeks. A new slogan for the city could be "Guayaquil: Where the animals pet YOU."

My memories will be atypical, however. The most common memory of Guayaquil is none at all because tourists tend to avoid this metropolis of over two million people. Most treat the city, the largest in Ecuador, as a necessary evil en route to a mojito-splashed tour of the Galapagos Islands. "Nothing to look at," they have been programmed to say. It's true that the city has worn out the novelty of concrete. And it's true that most of its buildings are less than a hundred years old, owing to the city's talent for catching fire every few years. (Or could it have been nature repeatedly attempting to purge a lumber-crusted lesion from its flesh?) To the architects' credit, however, many of the replacement structures have been tastefully rebuilt to appear much older, complete with arches and balconies from a car-free era. And I didn't find any colors reminiscent of a plastic fast food empire on them.

The city's current skyline may not boast a long and glorious pedigree stating that it survived such calamities as earthquakes, fires, sackings by pirates, and petty decisions by inbred royals. But Guayaquil can claim a homegrown enclave of well-adapted fauna (take that, Galapagos). Thinking of visiting? Make sure you bring enough peanuts for...well, everyone.

An Andean Equality

There are two premiums that many Ecuadorians often go without: privacy and silence.

It may be difficult for a Westerner used to such particulars to give them up, especially when arriving in a landscape where it is common to find three generations of a family—and their pets and chickens—magically shoehorned into a one-room cinderblock house. The constant din of chatter is the least of one's worries when compared to, say, roosters crowing at the rawest of hours, dueling jukeboxes jolting an entire valley until the bars run out of beer, or the diarrheic splattering of horn honks in place of traffic lights.

Nothing seems to personify the said deficits more than a ride on an Andean public bus. And I managed to heighten the effect—and hence the contrast—by taking one to a private spa. That's right, Melanie and I passed up a fancy gringo shuttle by taking the local transport from Quito, Ecuador, to the hot spring town of Papallacta.

Why? While the savings were of course significant (the public transportation cost ten times less), we could not put a price on the experience of jostling around for two hours with a microcosm of Ecuador. And the microcosm bore more variety than the size of the forty-five-seat, recycled coach might suggest. Take commerce, for instance. There is no need to bother with a trip to the market before your bus ride. The market comes to *you*. All it takes is a bus stop or a little traffic, and in climb the vendors. We hadn't even left Quito before we had the opportunity to procure a choice of four daily papers, ice cream cones, and plastic tubs of *seco de pollo* (juicy Ecuadorian stewed chicken, despite that the word *seco* means dry), with a rapid-fire sermon from a preacher thrown in for free.

In a curiously symbiotic relationship, Ecuadorian bus drivers tolerate the roving market. The vendors are never asked for a fare, and they always leave the next time the bus comes to a stop. But why would the driver complain? A customer slurping up fresh coconut juice from a plastic bag—delivered right to his seat—is a happy customer.

As towns of zinc-roofed houses crept by, a DVD of a Vicente Fernández movie skipped, froze, then skipped again on the television above the stairwell. The bus doubled as a school bus, scooping up giggly, uniformed children and dropping them off at a rate of one roughly every eleven feet. The stops allowed us to spy indigenous farmhands enjoying sprawled-out siestas on the hills. Their plump, floppy bodies lay motionless in a haphazard fashion as if they had suddenly collapsed after passing out from either a cholesterol-packed meal or a sleeping gas attack. At one of the longer standstills, we became acquainted with almost every straggly hair poking from a roadside pig. I found the bus's unhurried pace enjoyable when I noticed that it was handsomely calibrated to the speed of the landscape itself.

The absence of cows clinging to mountainsides signaled that we were climbing. While snaking through the groove of the Papallacta Pass at 13,400 feet, a woman sitting across from us asked us if we could close our window. She had wrapped her apple-shaped body in a typical dress for Ecuador's indigenous women of the Andes—a bundle of colorful fabric wrapped together in an overlapping puzzle. Pity that the woman's outfit didn't cover her hosed legs that popped out from the bottom of her dress.

I shan't label her a fashion victim, for the apparent sartorial non sequitur does have at least one practical use. On a recent visit to the Andean region of Peru, Ecuador's neighbor to the south, I had just exited a pay toilet and wandered up a narrow cobblestone side street, where a woman had lifted up her blanket frock and was straddling an Incan stone gutter in the center of the street. Despite breaking into a blush when our eyes met, she proved that the old Incan gutters still evacuate liquids with ease. And without having to peel off pants and undies, the time-saving, frock-lifting maneuver is perfect for peeing and running. Not to mention saving the one-sol (30¢) pay toilet fee.

Almost as fast as the pass arrived, it disappeared behind us, which meant arms grappled at the windows to open them again. The latch of our window, as with so many other windows on veteran Latin American coaches, was missing its plastic opening lever, leaving the rider with a stubby metal latch. So I pinched open the metal hook of the latch and pushed. Nothing moved. I shoved the window harder to unstick it, and it opened in a savage *shoooofff*. As the air curled in, I noticed that my middle finger was now missing its knuckle skin. I waved the hand in front of me, staring at amazement at the finger that was still in that brief limbo after it had been skinned and before it had decided to start bleeding. Where had that skin run off to?

I noticed a little pink flag flapping on the sharpness of the window latch's metal coupler, a darkly amusing development that Sylvia Plath could have appreciated after penning her poem "Cut."

I assumed that the riders of private vans arrived at the spa with perfect knuckles. And they had probably arrived a lot faster than we did. But before I counted them as the lucky ones when the bus dropped us off at the turnoff for the spa, I noticed the town of Papallacta, fresh for exploration, peeking up from below the cliff of the highway's bank. Since private vans drive straight to the spa, the guests inside the van would never know that the town existed. Melanie and I decided we would check it out to see how the Papallactans enjoy the natural gift of hot springs in their public baths in town.

But the visit to the town would be after we had sampled the offerings of the spa, the offerings that we'd saved up for. And that's when we crossed the line from public to private, which was not simply a chain-link fence that rung the manicured compound. The clerk strapped neon wristbands onto our hands, the kind you must wear at all-inclusive hotels or psychiatric wards. Every time we walked between our cabin and the main hotel, groundskeepers kept checking for the presence of our wristbands to make sure freeloaders—or worse, townies from below—hadn't breached the perimeter.

But the compound wasn't designed to require much walking around. The cabins all surrounded a tiled set of curved pools that piped in water from the area's thermal springs. The architects had built many little nooks among the pools' tiles and rocks, inside which you could simmer yourself in the mineral-rich water without even seeing another person, other than your lover. Thus we had achieved both premiums: privacy and silence, the latter making a scant exception for the burbling of the water as it circulated around the pool. With such a pampering under the glow of a snowcapped mountain, who would want to visit a nearby town with its crowded public pools?

We did, actually. If not for their pools, then for at least for a meal in a restaurant in town. I feel I haven't actually been somewhere unless I dine on what the locals are having, an action that lets a locale communicate nonverbally, opening a window into a way of life through the sensations of the tongue and gullet. What grows locally? What, if anything, is slaughtered regularly? A dinner plate can be an ephemeral message cast through the prisms of climate and habit. Few things can place a place like a taste bud or a whiff.

We walked down to the fence (after being stopped a few times to show our wristbands), and asked the guard to open the gate so we could walk to town. But the young guard twisted his face and paused as if he thought we were confused. His single word response, "Closed," trailed off limply into the night, as if he were not convinced of his own answer.

So instead, we dined at the hotel, the only place inside the sealed grounds where we could dine. As expected, the menu emphasized a sophisticated international theme. We had a pork loin accompanied by a concentrated sauce reduction, the kind you might find at a trendy Lower East

Side restaurant and served by a budding actress with an asymmetric haircut. Ecuadorian cuisine, like *vino hervido*, or boiled wine, made an occasional appearance on the menu, albeit after being upgraded. The common vino hervido in Ecuadorian cafes often smells of wino breath, and it is boiled to make it more palatable. The wine used at the spa's restaurant was so good it was a shame it had to be heated.

I thought travel writer Tom Miller had been exaggerating in his book *The Panama Hat Trail* when he kept encountering horrible instant coffee in Ecuador, an irony since Ecuador grows some of the best coffee beans in South America. (The good stuff usually ends up exported.) Twenty years after he wrote the book, and despite the fact that Ecuador has recently served as the setting for hideous "reality" television plots featuring casts who can't tell *patos* from *putas*, the coffee served at neighborhood eateries is still instant.

But here at the spa, the country within a country, we drank the smooth, freshly brewed pride of Ecuador itself. Indeed, the coffee reminded me of dining in New York. Or was it Los Angeles? Or Madrid? All the while, I thought of a reality that only globalization could provide: folks outside the fence, living not far from some of the most esteemed coffee plantations in the hemisphere, were spooning out cheap instant coffee that had been imported.

THE NEXT MORNING, we exited the gates and reentered the realm of public Ecuador. For us, this meant flagging down a Quito-bound bus whose interior awarded riders with the dankness of old sneakers. The ceiling-mounted speakers squeezed out tinny *campesino* ballads about losing one's cows or lover or money.

On one side of the road, the mountains stared down at us, the brows of their craggy outcrops tightened in disapproval. On the other side, there was no pesky guardrail to get in the way of the plunging view down the cliff and into the valley below. I marveled at the number of wooden crosses, signifying accidents involving generous amounts of haste and gravity, staked on the cliff side. But I was not surprised that the accidents happened; I was wondering how the crucifixes got staked out on the cliff without the staking party themselves falling over the edge. Perhaps that was why there were so many crosses.

The bus entered a series of innard-kneading curves. On a tight turn, the bus coasted to a stop. I had initially interpreted the act as a merciful maneuver; perhaps the driver was allowing the riders a chance to get off the bus and throw up that *vino hervido* without catching their seatmates in the crossfire. But I noticed that the bus began crawling past a van that had flipped onto its side and was straddling both lanes. Because of the vehicle's unnatural position, I could not read the markings on the van. Judging from its cleanliness, shape, and factory-new paint job, it looked hauntingly similar to the private vans used to shuttle tourists from the capital to the spa. It could have been the very vehicle we had passed up.

As we sailed into Quito's outskirts, I sipped from a bag of coconut juice and reflected that no matter how many comfy amenities you've managed to score, the Andes—in all their brutally unyielding permanence—will just as keenly swallow you up.

Beyond a Shadow of a Snout: a Saturday in Otavalo

Throughout rural Latin America, I have grown accustomed to navigating by sight—using landmarks—since street signs are usually viewed as needless luxuries. The Andean town of Otavalo, Ecuador, encouraged a new approach, however; it was the first place that allowed me to navigate by sound.

I first heard a trickle of shrieks bouncing down the street. Then a decisively savage grunt. I found this unsettling but reassuring. The auditory beacons assured me that I was walking in the right direction to reach Otavalo's early morning animal market, just off the Pan-American Highway.

At least the field near the highway was where the weekly market was supposed to take place. Convincing various hoofed animals to enter the field was a different matter. Cows parked their seven hundred pounds on the highway and mooed in protest. Hairy pigs wailed with anxiety as they were dragged toward the gate. Hoofs don't score much traction on pavement, but one pig managed to dig in, which only earned him a kick in his ham to drive him along.

"*Siga, siga*"—keep moving, keep moving—barked a lone policeman as he snapped his arms in unheeded calisthenics, a ghost in a pretty uniform. Because of such livestock gridlock, some of the transactions shamelessly went down along the highway instead of in the field, and saved the buyers the fifty-cent tax on all purchases.

I joined the rest of the creatures edging toward the gate, their heads bobbing downward, as we entered the narrows of the entrance. Being part of such a slow tide congregating towards an open field, I felt the odd sensation that I was part of a Woodstock-like gathering. The Woodstock in Vegetarian Hell, perhaps.

As over a hundred animals from several genera waited in a cramped formation, a twanging tension circulated around the grounds, tension that seemed to toy with the edges of chaos, panic, and rebellion. Bulging cow eyes attempted to size up the morning as tongues licked quivering stalactites of drool off snouts. Every groan and bovine emanation seemed to ratchet up the confusion. Was that last cry the cue for the subjugated to band together and fight their captors? Or was it simply another wry commentary? Those were a few thoughts that burbled about when I considered that, collectively, the animals easily outweighed their human handlers.

I glanced through the crisp morning air at the valley framed by the barren mounds of the Andes. Below, a sea of farmers grasped ropes that secured their bounty as buyers circled. The shoppers' feet—some wearing shoes, others not—indifferently churned a mixture of lamb, cow, and pig manure into the field. Its pungency was only held in check by the coolness of the early hour.

While the buyers fertilized the grounds, what did they look for in a prospective animal? I asked a squinting villager, who was in search of a pig, what his criteria were.

"The fat ones," he insisted.

The field offered all kinds of porcine permutations: young, old, hairy, extra hairy, and of course fat. Feel free to mix and match.

The market was not a show for tourists, however. After all, cows don't tend to be easily transportable souvenirs. The gathering wasn't part of a new trend; the Otavalo region has been holding livestock markets for over 100 years. The market's location is no coincidence, either, because the region claims a history of commerce, especially in textiles, that predates the Incas.

Ironically, the Otavalans' very skills would lead to their hardship for centuries. When the Incans arrived in the late 1400s and recognized the ability of the area's weavers and itinerant merchants, the Incans rewarded said talent by subjugating the weavers into labor obligations. Never one to miss an opportunity to exploit indigenous labor, the Spanish Empire slaughtered its way up the Andes and became the Otavalans' new bosses fifty years later. To insure each indigenous weaver produced his or her quota of work for the Spanish crown, the Otavalans' new lords chained many of the weavers to the looms.

Despite a workers' uprising in 1777 during which the indigenous sacked haciendas and wasted a few crooked clerics, the perpetual serfdom continued—even after Ecuador gained independence. The recipient of labor obligations simply shifted from the ousted Crown to the powerful oligarchy. Indigenous labor obligations were only abolished in 1857, two years after Ecuador abolished black slavery.

But the oligarchy ended up owning most of the valley, so for them it was business as usual—that is, profiting by abusing their employees. In 1964, however, Ecuador, fearing a communist revolution, passed the Law of Agrarian Reform, which smashed up large landholdings and finally enabled the indigenous of the area to own land that they worked.

It didn't take long for indigenous Otavalans to combine their land ownership with the skills the Otavalans have maintained throughout the generations, creating a rarity in the Western world: a prosperous indigenous community. Today, Otavalo, a town whose province of Imbabura is still seventy percent indigenous, even has an indigenous mayor.

And speaking of prosperity, when I crossed town after departing the field along the Pan-American Highway, I became entangled in the second of Otavalo's markets—the crafts bazaar, which showcased the area's ever-evolving weaving skills. Originating from the Plaza de Ponchos in the town's center, the crafts market appears every day, but on Saturday it spirals out onto the streets of Otavalo, forming a grid of colorful fabric, ceramics, and woven hats.

Rows of imitation shrunken heads, emulating the now-retired practice of the Shuar, one of Ecuador's Amazonian tribes, awaited modern-day trophy collectors. While breastfeeding Otavalo's newest generation, scarf vendors in ornate blouses simultaneously haggled with tourists from North America, Europe, neighboring Colombia, and even Quito. Thus the Otavalans were continuing their tradition, begun since long before Incan times, of creating goods for faraway buyers, although materials, image motifs, and technology have adapted along the way. Anybody want to buy a hand-sewn Castro doll?

But the crafts market merely remains a meatless eye in a vortex of carnivorous lust, for at the other end of town, the elbow-to-beak crowd of the small animal market, the place to buy and sell fowl and other critters that can fit in your hands, was already in full whirl when I approached. Fur and feathers eddied above the haggles like curse-filled word balloons. Crammed onto the confines of a narrow side street, the market swallowed me up as I entered, spitting me out next to a vendor holding a burlap bag filled with guinea pigs. She held one up by the back of its neck to show the shoppers the goods. *"Cuyes, cuyes!"* she yelled. Guinea pigs, guinea pigs! "Two dollars for a small, three-fifty for a large. A large feeds two people."

It was all about the grip. Next to me, a guinea pig squirmed free from another vendor and hastened its valiant escape attempt. The animal bounced off the road and spun its claws—like in the cartoons, I'm pretty certain—but since the shoppers were lined up so thickly, the guinea pig didn't get very far before it was scooped up and returned to its canvas purgatory. *"Siga, siga,"* another uniformed ghost sighed from somewhere.

I passed pens jammed with turkeys, ducks, and chickens—all three participants in a turducken, that Cajun monstrosity of meat. The birds couldn't have stood any closer together without becoming said dish (minus the Cajun cornbread stuffing).

Keeping a couple of roosters from escaping required other techniques, namely tying the two of them together. Since roosters don't care much for each other's company, this arrangement must have been uncomfortable for the fellows. But that didn't stop them from attempting a semi-concerted effort to flap away from the top of the box they had been placed upon. Because of their awkward, twined-up aerodynamics, however, they only succeeded in falling off the box, still tied together, of course.

The twine technique proved popular for whatever animals were for sale. If a vendor was selling a chicken and a kitten, he tied them together. Rabbits found themselves bound to roosters. The pattern seemed to be that a vendor would tie animals together that are of roughly the same size and weight.

The kittens, like the puppies, were sold as pets. I passed a man indulging his morning's purchase, a furry little puppy, in a gentle embrace. He crooned in a falsetto voice normally reserved for talking to infants, as he smothered the puppy with terms of endearment ending in the Spanish diminutive ending "–ito," not exactly the expected treatment of a future flank steak. The guinea pigs, however, left the market in canvas bags.

As for most of the other chirping and squeaking purchases, I found their logical endgame at the Otavalo food market, the fourth and final piece to Otavalo's Saturday buzz. Abutting the southern flank of the crafts vendors, a piecemeal roof invited me into alleys of stalls, some stacked with sacks of spices, others displaying tire-sized chunks of lard. Knuckles of some hoofed animal burbled in oil, and *arroz con pollo* (rice with chicken) bounced around in hot frying pans.

Each stall claimed its own specialty, including one that served crab. The Otavalans, like successful people everywhere, desire gastronomic variety, and have acquired a taste for some dishes they can't get locally, in this case shell-fish that is shipped from the coast. Feeding this passion, men in dress shirts wander the streets of the valley and sell live, flailing crabs instead of the expected haul of bootleg DVDs.

I wanted to test this curious culinary diversity along with Melanie, who earlier had elected to pass on the animal markets. Pacing ourselves on the deluge of Ecuador's meat-heavy cuisine, we gravitated toward the crab stall. The stall proved popular—there were no open seats—but a cook at a stall next door offered to fetch us her neighbor's crab soup (complete with a whole crab bathing inside). Forget nut-crackers—we were given fat wooden mallets. We just closed our eyes and hammered away at our sweet $3 find.

Clams also find themselves way above high tide—8,300 feet above sea level, to be exact—in a wok pan at yet another stall at the food market. We grabbed front row seats as Melanie asked the dexterous cook and owner of the stall, Lionel, what was in his clam stir-fry.

"Everything," he answered through a beckoning smirk. He was festooned with a lineup of seemingly incongruous shaker jars and raw shellfish. Would he attempt to mix them together? One of his hands tossed in the freshly shucked clams, another spooned in scoops of mustard and some other undisclosed spice, while his third and fourth arms—just blurs of sweat and skin—sprinkled in achiote seasoning and threw in shrimp. How did rice get in the pan already? Ah, the ol' sleight of hand.

Make no mistake, Otavalo is a proving ground for anyone who claims to be a carnivore. This reality is flaunted by the most popular item for lunch at the food market: roast pig. The whole thing. Some carcasses held cobs of *choclo*

(Andean large-kernel corn) in their mouths, while others just grinned at their embarrassingly low position in the food chain. Next to each carcass, I'd invariably find a customer pulling off chunks of crispy, oily skin from the pig head as if she were peeling a giant grapefruit. How does this self-service work, you ask? Pay just a dollar for an order of meat and you earn the right to peel off a piece of skin from the pig head. Go ahead, dig your fingers right in. You paid for it!

In the afternoon, Otavalo's meat fest finally went on a well-deserved hiatus, allowing us time to explore the delightfully clean little town. Guidebooks and tourists alike tend to label the town as nothing special to look at because there are few traditionally photogenic buildings. And since the gargantuan crafts market tends to be the singular attraction for most visitors, many may not have noticed that the enterprising Otavalans have reinvested some of their market income in the construction and appearance of their city. Red, blue, and yellow squares of masonry—the three colors of the Ecuadorian flag—form the sidewalks. Multi-paneled, varnished wooden doors are all the rage. Ornate lampposts create downtown scenes reminiscent of small town America. One of the main thruways even has a bike lane.

But the most interesting quality of life enhancements are the town's garbage trucks. That's right, garbage trucks. They're the vehicles whose mechanical guts earn them universal derision elsewhere for not having evolved far past the first few earsplitting grinds of the industrial age.

While garbage and recycling trucks regularly prowl Otavalo to keep the town looking its best, the trucks also place something back on the curb—they tinkle out gentle, pentatonic melodies to keep the town sounding its best too. It's as if each truck's innards hid a spinning music box, plinking one chiming note at a time while secretly crushing bottles. I wanted to litter just so one of the trucks would swoop by and play me a tune.

I would soon procure an honest fix of music at the restaurant Mi Otavalito, where a band squeezed in between tables and swayed to their renditions of Andean folk music. The music—carried by flutes, guitars, vocals, and a large side drum—sounded familiar to me. That is because for the past few decades, Otavalan bands have been traveling outside Ecuador and performing on city sidewalks from New York to Amsterdam. Live bands are yet another of Otavalo's commodities for worldwide export. Musicians from other Andean nations such as Bolivia have even gone so far as to wear their hair long like the Otavalans in order to pass for them.

But we didn't go to the restaurant just for its musical ambience. Remember all those guinea pigs sold at the small animal market? We had a dinner date with one of them. He arrived a little after we did, and was dressed in the most typical fashion: a coat of oven-roasted spices. With his tiny joints and thick skin, he made us work for our meal. If you've never eaten cuy, may I recommend that you ask for extra napkins?

The setting sun signaled the end of the markets. No more animals, right? Well, for some, the night was just beginning. In Otavalo, Saturday night is cockfight night. As with the town's business acumen and its architecture, Otavalo takes its cockfighting seriously. They built an entire palace devoted to the sport, complete with stadium seating, a roof, and storage cages for the fighters of the evening.

According to the betting board, hundreds of dollars in wagers awaited the outcome of multiple rounds of male angst. The ring itself, lined with a thin red rug to lessen the visible traces of past skirmishes, is about eighteen feet in diameter, but clearly, there's only enough room for one cock. To insure a dose of entertainment for the $1 price of admission, the rooster handlers securely taped two-inch metal spikes to the ankles of each fighter.

When the evening's announcer stepped into the ring, the gathering hushed, save for the intermittent squawking of roosters locked up in cages in back of the ring. Each of the two first-round handlers shoved his rooster into the other rooster's face to get the anger flowing. And then they were released. Neck feathers flared wide like inflatable pool toys. As the handlers crouched down inside the ring and forcefully whispered commands to their fighters, the destruction began.

The ring swirled with the damp scent of a chicken coop. Feathers flew in the air. Hearing and smelling the excitement below, the caged roosters worked themselves up into a crescendo of screeching, a chant-like ritual.

There seemed to be only two rules. The first is that if the claws of one rooster become snagged in the feathers of another, the handlers will untangle them. Secondly, the fight will only stop if either the twenty-minute buzzer goes off, or a fatality is racked up. In the first round that night, the buzzer sent both roosters from the ring bloody but lucid. The second round, however, awarded the crowd with a gladiator-style kill, without the gladiator-ring cheers. The ring fell into the silence of a funeral parlor.

It was unclear how the trainer of the deceased rooster planned to honor him. But I'm sure the town's food market had a few ideas.

Coup in a Cup: a Tale of Venezuelan Tipple

I've found that you can learn about a culture by looking at what they throw away. To see what Venezuela is drinking, for instance, you only need to gaze out the window while cruising down the highway. Like runway lights, empty bottles of beer and 80-proof aguardiente (along with a token water bottle) ushered me along as I traveled in a taxi through the hills of the western Lara state.

I am not implying that all Venezuelans are drunk-driving litterbugs, although both littering and drunk driving remain serious problems. If you wish to keep a gruesome tally concerning the latter issue, just count the crosses staked along the highway or browse local papers for pictures of the daily windshield blood.

Despite such devotion to drinking and multitasking, the lack of wine bottles scattered beside the pavement reinforced what I had been told about the tropical country:

wine is not very popular in Venezuela. Not surprisingly, accepted wisdom has declared the tropics terrible for growing wine-quality grapes.

"I only use wine for cooking," confessed my cab driver, his voice barely cutting over the radio's machine-gun chatter that covered the day's World Cup game.

I arrived in Venezuela at a dynamic time, however. Venezuelan president Hugo Chávez has not cornered the market on revolutions in the country, for wine could soon be liberated from the confines of the kitchen (and church services). Bodegas Pomar, a company in the scrub-covered mountains around the town of Carora, is not only making wine from grapes grown locally, but their grape haul is twice as large as that of temperate-zone wineries. Even more surprising: the wine is drinkable. We were headed to Carora in hopes that I could uncover how the company has been defying its own latitude for the past twenty years.

At first, the guard at the gate of Bodegas Pomar seemed more interested in commenting on America's poor World Cup showing than helping me find answers. "United States is eliminated!" he barked at me. Since soccer was temporarily trumping politics, I did not have to perform the usual task to which many Americans abroad can relate: the ceremonial disassociating of oneself from the George W. Bush regime. Therefore, I only needed to tender a little soccer, which is the currency of conversation in Venezuela during the World Cup. I decided to praise the performance of several Latin American teams. "How about the Brazilian team?" I asked. "They're so…"

My bullshit engine began to sputter, but the guard took my hesitation as a chance to excitedly finish my sentences for me. Something about the players being powerful yet graceful to watch, I think. Afterward, he was happy to arrange a meeting for me.

And thus I earned my chance to find out how the company hauls in that mutant grape yield. My cabbie tagged along. As he gazed at the neatly arranged bottles in glass cabinets along the walls of the showcase room, I imagined that he was wondering why someone would pay over ten dollars for something that's used to make beef gravy.

Before arriving, I had read that the company harvests grapes twice a year (temperate-zone wineries only have one harvest per year), which would account for the doubling. But how do they do it? At the company's showcase room desk, salesperson Almudena Gutierrez retired my inquiry quickly. "Because there is no winter," she answered. "That is why we have two harvests a year: once in March, and another in September." Ah, yes. The tropical curse on grapevines has now been turned into an advantage, thanks to a little horticultural cleverness and a lucky, semi-arid climate.

Labor laws of Venezuela do not apply to grapevines, since the vines only get one month of rest every six months, and then they have to start cranking out more grapes. But when you think of it, don't the wine experts always scream about grapes making better wine if the vines are stressed?

It takes more than a monster yield to make wine, however. The quality of the grapes is suitable for winemaking because the valley where the grapes grow becomes a little cool at night, tricking the vines into thinking that they've been happily photosynthesizing along the Rhone River in France. That temperature variation ends up bestowing the grapes with the right sugar content for winemaking, even though the vines are only ten degrees north of the equator.

With such an agricultural innovation, you'd think the young company would be keen on offering samples of their drink. Any visitor to, say, Napa Valley or the Finger Lakes region of New York expects to stroll into a winery and be festooned with a flight of glasses for tasting. Even at Venezuela's own rustic markets, stalls of aguardiente-pimping vendors will swiftly thrust a plastic cup in your hand so you may sample their clear, artisan swill. But not at the winery. The company only offers tours and tastings during their dual harvesting months of March and September. I visited in June.

But I can hardly blame Bodegas Pomar. To give tours to visitors, you need more than tour guides, you also need visitors. Despite Carora's storybook-quaint colonial buildings and narrow, centuries-old streets that would make vacationing Americans involuntarily pause and sigh, I didn't see any tourists—American or otherwise—in Carora. Nor in the nearby city of Barquisimeto. If the company adds a daily wine tasting to the area's collection of craft markets that hawk everything from pottery to carvings, the Barquisimeto area could become a natural tourist lure. (Is Venezuela's Ministry of Tourism reading this?)

It certainly doesn't help that wine is not terribly popular among the working class of Venezuela, despite the fact that Pomar's lowest-tier bottle goes for B11,000 ($5) in the liquor stores, about what you'd pay for a bottle of aguardiente. Their mid-range bottles of tasty, cherry-like Petit Verdot cost B23,000 ($11). But the company, keeping in mind Venezuelan tastes, has already started marketing the latter as great for accompanying goat in coconut broth, one of the specialties of the region.

While wine and goat may still remain an unfamiliar dinner pairing, the grapes themselves are popular. Along the highway between Carora and Barquisimeto, dozens of vendors have set up identical stands hawking boxes of grapes harvested from the area. Could a wine trend be the next logical step? Watch the empties along the side of the road for future developments.

The following week, at the other end of the country, I would discover that the Venezuelan wine revolution has an ally, albeit grapeless. Using the city of Maturín as a base, I took another taxi and braved the spaghetti-thin turns of mountain roads up to Caripe, a town in the eastern Monagas state. My destination was the store El Palacio de las Fresas (Palace of the Strawberries), purveyor of fruit wines.

After a little obligatory soccer banter (I nodded in astonishment during each mention of an extra time period), I met a vibrant man named Rigoberto Duque Sierra, who ferments and bottles everything from coffee beans to passion fruit, all fortified with a little sugar. He even ages his blackberry and strawberry wines in oak barrels, just like what is done to the familiar, grape-based classic.

But according to Rigoberto, his wines, which he has been making for over twenty years, are more than alcoholic drinks. As he lined up his roster of bottles atop the store's wooden counter, he launched into a dizzying run-down detailing each bottle's special power.

"This one is medicine," he said while cradling a bottle of ginger wine. "It will kill a headache in five minutes! Here. Try some." (Without having a headache at the time, I could not vouch for its effectiveness.)

His brother, a chiropractor and a traditional medicines practitioner, has supplied several of the wine recipes that

Rigoberto follows, including one for a medley of herbs that will cure the flu. In a low, devilish whisper, Rigoberto pointed out that his rose petal wine "is a strong aphrodisiac. It works in half an hour!"

His wine, at B10,000 ($4.50) per bottle, didn't seem to clean my intestines—nor make me burp up irresistible pheromones. But I discovered later on that his coffee and cacao wines tasted great when I poured them over vanilla ice cream. At the least, I did my part to support wine's unlikely attempt at a rise to power in a tropical country. But I still doubt that corks will challenge the popularity of kicks.

Magic Scrap

When a twenty-year-old, rusted car in the States becomes unfashionable, the owner usually unloads it and begins to talk about it in the past tense. Think the car is dead? Think again. That same vehicle just might still be cruising on cheap gas on the mountain highways of Venezuela.

Or at least a fender of it.

Venezuela's automobiles never seem to die. They hobble along with whatever prosthetic replacements arrive via container shipments from the States.

The South American country's thrifty car culture developed thanks to the rise and fall of Venezuela's oil fortunes. In 1973, the price of oil quadrupled, spurring a Venezuelan spending spree. The country's rising middle class engorged itself on American-made cars. When oil prices fell in the mid-1980s, new car purchases became rare. While Cuba's roads are viewed as a time capsule of America in the 1950s,

Venezuela's roads are, for the most part, frozen in the 1980s.

Thus, Venezuelan highways remain the domain of leprous Chevy Novas and boxy Buicks with black eyes. On some of the older cars, the replacement bumpers still wear the bumper stickers of their unwitting American donors, which lead to sightings of traffic-bound Caracas autos declaring "My Child Is a Springfield Honor Roll Student." If I ignored the stunning mountain scenery—and the occasional, shiny SUV—I almost expected to hear the latest Men at Work song shooting from the radio. The acrid scent of the Cold War seemed to waft back in. And I could have sworn I saw a mullet or two…

But a visit to a car-parts dealer sobered me up. My taxi driver, owning the road in his 1987 Buick Century (a late model for Venezuela, apparently), informed me that he needed to make a quick pit stop to procure a new windshield washer fluid container. The dealer he visited only sold American car parts. An acre of them. Walking among the rows of neatly sorted bumpers, headlights, and grills for Chevys and Fords, I could not help but to think of the place as a showcase of my country's car-centered psyche—dissected. Not maliciously, but lovingly. Who else would preserve an era that America's consumption culture discarded years ago?

And since the government subsidizes gasoline prices (reducing its cost to a quaint twelve cents per gallon, the lowest on the planet), there does not seem to be any reason to trade in that old fuel hog for a newer model. Besides, if you did, your child would no longer be an honor roll student.

Liming Lessons

Sometimes, the best introduction to a cradle of wholesome nature is through a plastic pipe. It poked from the greenery of the mountainside, although I hadn't noticed it until we'd stopped. Cool water fell from the pipe, water that I drank at the insistence of someone I had met an hour ago. I was standing along a single-lane road that snaked through the mountains above Port of Spain, Trinidad, while Juan, my cab driver, thrust his bottle under the shooting arc of water for a refill.

Juan, who had just picked me up at the airport, told me he always stops at the spring when he crosses to the north, and that the water is safe. The creek flows so high in the island's lush strip of mountains across its northern coast that humanity has not had a chance to foul it up. But humanity was not far behind. A discarded fried chicken box, crumpled and faded, sat by the pavement.

He had parked along a guardrail-free edge affording a vista of the valley that cut down to Port of Spain. It revealed

an obsessively trim golf course, stair-stepped condos working their way down to the coast, and a V-shaped view of the
Caribbean Sea, where a lone oil tanker seemed motionless
in the calm waters, a modest reminder of one of the island's
main sources of wealth. I tried to avoid thinking about the
head-on collision whose aftermath we had just crept past a
few minutes before, and how much more horrific it could
have been had it occurred at this curve. Instead, I looked
over the side of the road, where a patch of staked tomato
plants gripped the deep slope descending south. Perhaps
the patch's gardener would use rappelling gear at harvest
time.

Juan aimed the bottle at me. "Have more if you would
like." Black tassels of his corkscrew perm bounced when he
nodded. He had round, muscular shoulders uncommon for
someone who spends most of his day in a bucket seat. FLU-
ENT IN SPANISH AND NORWEGIAN read his business card,
owing to his part-Venezuelan heritage and his years of
chauffeuring in Norway, adding to Trinidad's mixture of
African, South Asian, French, and British legacies. Juan's
multiethnic nurturing reminded me of a line from a vintage
1961 *Holiday Magazine's Travel Guide to the Caribbean*, referring to Trinidad as "a melting pot to end all melting pots."

Just a few days before, I was walking in the Trinidadian
neighborhood of South Richmond Hill in my hometown of
Queens. Living in America's most diverse county, I am
blessed to be able to travel around a microcosm of the
world, visiting the outposts of those who have recently arrived, neighborhoods that gradually change the face of
America.

I have noticed little evidence of the stress of New York
City attaching itself to South Richmond Hill. I have never

seen anyone run madly toward the subway stop while cursing along the way, never a grocery store customer abusing checkout clerks like invisible domestic help, no one fighting over a cab, no power lunches held in the restaurants. I doubt that Trinidadians are immune—as people shape the city, the city shapes the people—but I could not help but suspect there was something particular about South Richmond Hill's unflappability I had been witnessing.

Keeping in mind my experiences in the Queens neighborhood's spice stores, restaurants, and CD shops, many of which were drawing in patrons through steady streams of chutney—a musical fusion of a dancehall reggae beat under an Indian vocal melody—I had decided to travel to where it all originated.

Now here I was in Trinidad, drinking untreated, freely running water. Fluids were prudent since we were headed down to the humidity of sea level on the northern side of the range. I had asked Juan to take me to his favorite beach-side lunch stand of Maracas Bay. No gastronomic trip to the Bay would be complete, he assured me, without first stopping at a cliff-side kiosk overlooking the Bay for a snack of tamarind candy. Under Juan's tutelage, I asked for it "with pepper" to have it with chili seasoning. A surprise seed lurked inside each tangy ball, waiting to crack a tooth if the treat were eaten with haste.

We descended between two shaggy green fingers of land jutting from the coast to arrive at Maracas Bay, where several tent-covered kitchens near the beach were frying up sandwiches of breaded kingfish and shark. Juan brought me to Nathalie's, where Nathalie herself, her hair in a polka-dotted silk wrap, beamed a big smile at Juan and started teasing him about recent events in his social life. While airing playful suspicion of Juan's shapely girlfriend having buttock implants, she fished the fried bread out of an oil-filled wok with a skimmer. Juan denied the charge, countering with a description of his girlfriend's workout routine, something involving one hundred fifty reps of lunges and squats per day. Our shark 'n' bakes were ready.

The shark 'n' bake is a Trinidadian sandwich in which nothing is baked. Both the shark and the bread are fried, and the word bake has long since been repurposed by the Trinidadians to mean bread. As for the shark, it may also be a misnomer. I had been warned that several of the shark 'n' bake stands at Maracas Bay do not serve it anymore due to cost and overfishing, replacing it with any common white fish but still keeping the name of the sandwich the same. I could not say with certainty whether she served us shark, but after I dressed the sandwich with *chadon beni* (a condiment made with culantro), tamarind sauce, hot sauce, leafy lettuce, and deep red tomatoes from her open fixin's table, I didn't care much for controversy.

TRINI TO DE BONE read the menu neatly painted on a piece of sheet metal hanging behind the counter. An electrical outlet above the counter dangled from the concrete wall, looking strangled. With propane flames under the woks, the stand had little use for electricity anyway.

I glanced out at the waves rolling into Maracas Bay, and noticed right away why it is a popular afternoon escape from Port of Spain: postcard palm trees; Afro-Trinidadians and Indo-Trinidadians spiking beach balls, sharing shark 'n' bakes, adjusting bikini tops and bottoms. Plenty of buttocks for Nathalie to consider. A few groups of Muslim women, espousing a curious sartorial adaptation, arrived at the beach in above-the-knee skirts, short sleeve shirts, and head shawls, ready to enjoy the scenery and the scene.

At the western end of the crescent, wooden fishing boats bobbed in the surf in front of a small village. The shark fillets, I figured, don't have too far to travel, if they are still being caught at all. I was interested in learning more about such convenience, so Juan walked with me to the village, where he found Nicolas, a friend of his, sitting on a low concrete bridge. Nicolas had already returned from six hours of fishing just outside the bay. His lean, bare chest curled inward as he sat with us. Gesturing with his bottle of Carib beer for us to join him, he wore a contented half-smile, suggesting a successful afternoon at sea.

The naming of a beer after the island's indigenous nation, the Caribs, seemed a little out of touch at first. But coming from the States, where the First Nations have found their tribal names hijacked for use on everything from jeeps to attack helicopters, I figured that a First Nation's name appearing on a beverage encouraging social interaction and relaxation might be an improvement.

A round of cold Caribs appeared from somewhere and was placed into our hands. When I asked Nicolas if he had noticed a dip in the shark population, he told me that they were still catching shark, plenty of shark. Had he already sold his shark to the stalls on the other side of the beach? Perhaps the shark I had eaten had been hoisted up into his boat? "The shark we catch are too small," he said. "We sell them to Port of Spain. Sometimes when the vendors over here run out, they run down to us to buy more." But where, then, do the shark 'n' bake vendors regularly procure their shark? He waved his hand towards the mountains. "They buy larger shark from Port of Spain."

I tried to digest the dynamics of the Trinidadian shark's hectic back-and-forth landlubbing, which added to the fish's intrigue and alleged elusiveness on the Maracas Bay menu. A young wife of another fisherman overheard my questions and showed me the view screen of a point-and-shoot digital camera that held a picture of her four-year-old son straddling a hawksbill turtle on the beach. He was attempting to ride it like a pony. The woman's husband, after fishing for shark, had caught the turtle in the Bay a few days before. She advanced to the next file on the memory card, a video of the turtle being butchered with a machete. I had difficulties understanding her accent during the narration, but I gathered that the resulting dinner involved soup with a coconut broth. Her son, who I recognized as the turtle jockey, kept throwing pop snappers onto the pavement next to the bridge, punctuating her story with piercing cracks.

I looked for a recycling bin for the empty Carib. Nicolas pointed to the sand under the bridge, where a collection of bottles had already been congregating in the dried-up creek bed. I hesitated, but eventually added mine. Not all detritus on the beach was detritus, however. Underneath a few palm trees, a kitchen refrigerator, rusted and turned onto its back, appeared to be a piece of abandoned rubbish, but it was actually filled with bags of ice and served as storage for fish before they made their way to Port of Spain markets.

Another sweating bottle of Carib was placed into my hand. It seemed that everyone driving or walking by us stopped for a chat. This choke point along the narrow, one-lane bridge provided a perfect excuse for hanging out, the cherished pastime that the Trinidadians call liming. Of all the Trinidadian English terms, I found liming the most fascinating, perhaps due to one popular etymology of the word that pegs its origins to the British colonial period. Upon observing how the British—known as Limeys—were standing around, chatting and doing nothing, the Trinidadians found the pastime worth mimicking. So the Trinidadians honored their colonial overlords by naming the enjoyable activity after them.

Turtle Jockey's mom asked me about snow in my hometown of New York. She had never seen snow before. "It must be nice," she said above the cracks of snappers at our feet. It was two weeks before Christmas, and I had already spotted manger scenes decorating lawns of headquarters of multinational gas and oil companies and blow-up snowmen atop hardware store awnings in Port of Spain. I can understand her desire to suspend the island's usual climate for just a day to experience a little bit of winter. But I told her how snow in New York City is a plague because there are few places to move the stuff; and then there is the overabundance of absentee landlords who don't clear the snow in front of their properties, allowing the sidewalks to turn into skating rinks. She laughed but still seemed a bit wistful.

Besides shark, Nicolas had brought in kingfish and *carit* (mackerel). On a good day, he said, he could make 2000 Trinidad and Tobago dollars, about $320. "There are good days and bad days," he added.

Nicolas gave Juan a cardboard box carrying four of the fish he had caught that day. When Juan and I began the drive back to Port of Spain, I mentioned to him that Nicolas—liming, buying rounds of Caribs, giving away fish—

must have had been celebrating a bountiful catch that afternoon. "He is always like that," Juan said.

His words began to stir something else within him, and after a pause, he continued, "Stress is bad for the heart. Why have stress? Just chew it off, mon."

The sun had sunk under the horizon in its usual tropical freefall, as if it had decided it had worked enough today. The only light came from headlights darting towards us and passing us on the right, an unsettling feeling for an American accustomed to right-side driving. I kept thinking about the head-on accident we had seen earlier, and how someone driving back from a big lime, a dozen Caribs sloshing around in his veins, could emerge from a curve a little too sloppily, which wouldn't take much on a narrow road such as this.

Only now had I begun to allow Juan's words, in all their attractive simplicity, to soak in. For the rest of the ride through the mountains, I kept my window open, listening to frogs chirping as they began to own the jungle evening.

THE NEXT AFTERNOON, I was pondering the etymology of doubles—a chickpea-loaded, pepper-spiked street sandwich in a thick, crepe-like wrap. Just as you can never have a singular inning in cricket, you can never have a singular double at the street food stalls of Trinidad. Does this relatively new Trinidadian English term mimic a British exception to its own language's grammar?

I'd had a doubles for lunch back home in Queens, and had thought I could find it more easily in Trinidad. But all I could do was imagine the word's history because all the doubles had disappeared, along with their vendors, by late morning.

At breakfast time, I had been foolishly browsing the musty offerings of a used bookstore instead, asking myself how a yellowed 1981 video arcade game guide had found its way onto its shelves. Tips for avoiding ghosts in *Pac-Man*! How to protect your *Missile Command* cities! The bookstore clerk, a portly Indo-Trinidadian with a wiry beard, bobbed in a standing dance as he watched me walk farther into the store. A strange mania had widened his eyes. He called to me in quick, machine-gun phrases, none of which I understood, but the intonation indicated a response was requested. A radio behind him was pumping out a chutney song, and his posture twisted into the radio, as if the music had cast a magnetic field over his spine. Then I understood—he had been commenting on the lyrics. I recognized the track as a Christmas song I had heard before in the city's restaurants, just another ornament of Christmas in a country where no faith wants to be left out of the holiday's secular festivities.

After emerging from the store and failing to discover an open doubles stand, I ducked into a nearby roti shop. I would not be defeated, not completely. The counterwoman pointed out her *chana*, or chickpeas, in the steam table. She also served pieces of fried bread, and in another twist of Trinidadian nomenclature, she called them pies. The dangling flesh of her puffy arms jiggling to and fro, she cut one pie open and stuffed the chana inside with a little red pepper sauce. The late-riser's doubles.

I looked at her selection of fountain drinks and recalled how the city's restaurants have a fondness for adding a few drops of bitters to everything from rum punch to coleslaw. "Is your sea moss shake bitter or sweet?" I asked.

"Just right," she said as she handed me the shake through the metal grate separating the dining area from the cashier. It was sweet and easy to drink, with only a suggestion of watered-down crepe batter.

Instead of standing and eating the chana near a sidewalk doubles cart while exposed to the will of the Trinidadian sun, I sat in the shop while a groaning air conditioner dripped on my head. An agreeable trade.

I walked west to the neighborhood of St. James, where the weaving foot traffic along Western Main helped boost my count of Obama t-shirt sightings. A daughter in pigtails waddled next to her parents, each holding boxes of fried chicken and pointing into clothing store windows. Elsewhere, folded up mattresses were lugged, gold teeth revealed. Nikes, flip-flops, and bare feet all marched through the heavy heat of noon. Feeling the grip of thirst tighten, I bought a cold, bark-based drink known as *mauby*—its bitterness taking away some of its thirst-quenching ability— from a grocery store near where GOD FIGHTS THOSE WHO FIGHT AGAINST ME had been stylishly handwritten in baby-blue paint onto the side of a burger cart. Syrupy chutney songs escaped from stores, from car radios, from everywhere.

The chana pie had been small, and I began to look for a place to have another. Stacks of teapots and dancing Santas and remote-controlled cars choked the sidewalk, so I started up a side street. "Hey, Mr. White," a soft voice called to me from underneath a sign reading ST. JAMES MEAT COTTAGE AND SUPERMARKET. I looked down to find a drunkard lying against the wall. Only his head moved, as if a lazy puppeteer were manipulating the stick of his neck and nothing else. He gave me a welcoming nod, and then went back to his spaced-out stares. Even the bum was pleasant and cordial, in his own way. Chewing it off, he was.

I entered a suburban stretch of quiet concrete houses. The neighborhood had paid tribute to Indian cities in its street names: Bengal, Calcutta, Madras, Delhi—the cities from which the British had acquired indentured laborers whose ancestors now form forty percent of the country's population. Bombay Street brought me back to Western Main, where I ordered a second hit of chana, this time accompanying stewed *agouti* at Jazzie's Wildmeat Restaurant. At the steam table, the matronly owner scooped out on-the-bone chunks of the ten-pound jungle rodent, slow-cooked and immersed in a brown broth that was sweet and, not surprisingly, a little bitter.

I reflected on how impossible such an offering would be in the States with its phobia of eating anything from the rodent family, as if every rodent is just a subway rat in disguise. Meanwhile, here in Trinidad, the rich, pork-like meat on the little bones mixed freely on the plate with the spicy chickpeas, and I no longer thought about missing out on doubles. I had traded up to free range goodness with something I cannot find in the Trinidadian restaurants of Queens.

THE SKY GREW PURPLE and the frogs began their nightly concert. But they were not alone. Tinny bongs of a steel pan practice session floated down driveways of gabled Vic-

torian houses, the players as unseen as the frogs, challenging the frogs to a loose point and counterpoint that didn't
sound unpleasant.

I was still feeling numb from the puncheon I had just
drunk at a bar temptingly named Sweet Lime. Puncheon is
a liquid bludgeon so powerful that one cannot bring a bottle onto an airplane due to its flammable seventy-five percent alcohol content. I had asked the bartender to cut it
with coconut water, perhaps eliminating its flammability
but not its potency.

Thanks to the puncheon's involvement, I used extra cau-
tion crossing the streets, most of which were without traffic
lights. I was walking along Ariapita Avenue, home to many
of the capital's restaurants and nightclubs. To call the avenue a strip or a main drag would be misleading; active
storefronts sporadically dotted the avenue and on neighboring streets, as if each building, almost all of them free-
standing, demanded privacy from the others in a tranquil
take on urban life.

The establishments threw the occasional half-moon of
light onto the concrete sidewalks: backlit bar signs, neon-
fronted Chinese restaurants, interior lighting of a shop selling feathered and sequined Carnival bikinis modeled on
bronze-colored mannequins. On one long stretch between
clubs, GOD WANTS THE TRUTH had been stenciled onto a
shuttered house with a rusted roof. But no one else was
around to heed its warning. The sidewalks remained otherwise dark and empty. Most partygoers were driving to the
bars and restaurants, allowing me to follow the soft, sweet
bongs of stray steel pan notes after I turned into a side
street. Someone was warming up nearby.

I found the source: the panyard of the Invaders, the world's oldest steel pan ensemble. Port of Spain is the home of several panyards—outdoor practice spaces doubling as ensemble headquarters—and each December, the groups begin to practice for Carnival. The gate was open, and a handful of onlookers sat against a wall, a short strip of cracked pavement separating them from the band. The onlookers exuded the familiar patience of either family members or friends. When I approached them, one woman stood up and, serving as a makeshift bartender, sold me a Carib she had retrieved from a room behind her and told me the band would be starting practice in a few minutes.

Noticing my curiosity for the pans, each of which dangling on a rack to allow more resonation and isolation, a man appearing in his fifties approached me and waved me into one of the storage rooms. The man, Jim, showed me a pile of pans, tambourines, and a regular trap set, all waiting to be hauled out to the playing area as each player arrived for practice. "I play this," he said, digging out a polished ring of metal, a brake drum from a pickup truck, rechristened as an instrument known as an iron. He passed it to me. I wasn't ready for its dense weight as it dragged down on my arm.

He brought me into another of the group's storage rooms, where orderly rows of pans of various depths were lined up on racks. The pans, having been cut, polished, hammered with note bubbles, and painted, obscured their past lives as fifty-five-gallon oil drums. The storage room also told a story of its own past life: it was a shipping container, ribbed walls and all, now covered with purple paint. Openings for a door and a few windows had been cut into it.

As a drummer, I have often searched for fresh, emerging, evolving sounds. Hence the appeal of the steel pan. It's a relatively young instrument, having been born in the 1940s from the combination of colonialist oppression and the innovation of the oppressed. The government of the British colony of Trinidad and Tobago banned drumming on the island in 1884 for fear that the ex-slaves, who outnumbered the British fifty to one, could communicate through the drums and eventually pass secret messages that could lead to a revolt. Afro-Trinidadians began circumventing the drumming ban by using other items as percussion, such as tuned bamboo sticks, which the British ended up banning as well.

By the 1940s, Trinidadians began experimenting with tuning and playing the undersides of cookie tins. (I can just imagine youngsters pleading with their parents in the grocery store: We really don't want to load up on sugar, we just want the tin!) An American navy base on the island provided a surplus of used oil drums, and the musicians found that the oil drums provided a richer tone than that of a cookie tin. The larger size of oil drums also gave the Trinidadians the ability to hammer more notes per pan, allowing a single pan to produce a chromatic scale. After World War II, the British saw no point in clamping down on another form of musical expression during an inevitable tide of independence movements (Trinidad's arrived in 1962). The steel pan was born.

The sizes and note ranges of the various classifications of pans—tenors, cellos, bass—borrow their names from a realm normally associated with classical music. This is no surprise. Sure, they are fashioned from oil drums, but the steel pan is not a drum in the musical sense. It is a melodic instrument, an idiophone used to carry a tune rather than lay down a rhythm. The Invaders' trap drum set, conga, tambourines, and Jim's iron take care of the latter. Owing to an ensemble's full spectrum of notes, Shubert and Beethoven often find their way into repertoires in addition to the expected fiery calypso numbers, and even a mixture of the two.

I sat on a steel I-beam and watched about three dozen pan players launch into Michael Jackson's "Don't Stop 'til You Get Enough." Jim smiled to me as he tapped out sixteenth notes, accenting all the "and" notes instead of the downbeat on the edge of the brake drum's inner lip. The iron called out with a piercing bell sound, cutting across the ensemble whose pans had handily taken over all of the song's original melodic duties—those of the guitar, keyboard, horns, and vocals.

Pan players kept trickling in from the night, filling up the empty pans and carrying out conga drums from the storage room. The tenor players, carrying the vocal melodies, busily worked short, rubber-tipped sticks around the pans, appearing like chefs turning stir-fry in woks, all in theatrical synchronization. Jazz numbers and ballads showcased the bass pans, whose notes rung in tender bongs.

Jim sat with me on the I-beam during their break. "When will you start playing?" he asked.

I had mentioned to him earlier that I am also a drummer. "I think I'll just watch for tonight and see how it's done." When I asked him how long he had been with the band, he answered that he had only been playing with them regularly for a few years, since now he has more time that he is retired. I was surprised when he told me he was seventy years old—as old as the Invaders, as old as the steel pan.

I asked him when he started playing pans and the iron. He pointed to a toddler sitting near the wall. "Since I was as small as him." He dove into a story of when he would sneak out of his house and run to the Invaders' panyard and try to join in. "And I came back and got my teeth cut," he said with a hearty snicker.

He returned to the band lineup and ran through a set ending in an energetic rendition of "Hot Hot Hot." As much as I romanticized the Trinidadian-born instrument, I also found myself reflecting on what had been necessary for the steel pan—and the rest of modern Trinidad—to exist. The country bears the history of slavery, the same ignominious climate that preceded the genesis of blues, rock, and jazz in America, reggae in Jamaica, and candombe in Uruguay. Musical traditions that began in Africa did not arrive at the Americas willingly, and they not only survived, but blended with the new environment and evolved into defining threads of culture.

When I grew up wearing out Jack DeJohnette and Jimi Hendrix tapes, I always viewed the music as American. American like me. The connection between the music and the country's history was always there, just not exposed and illuminated in the way that only a direct experience can provide. The freshness of travel, of hearing the steel pan harmonies, of seeing delight on Jim's face as he tapped the iron, had drawn the two together, showing the depth of the forces that have shaped Trinidad's people. The term "melting pot" is normally used in a happy, worldly sense but, as with America, Trinidad began as a melting pot forged by force.

I cannot cease to wonder how a wretched social landscape could give birth to something so beautiful. It must require a particular attitude to see it through—a confident ability to chew off adversity along the way.

I looked out to the street, and several people had gathered on a balcony opposite the panyard for a prime view. The band was between tunes, and the frogs took advantage, sneaking in a few chirping volleys, refusing to deprive themselves of song.

Intermission #1: The Ballet of the San Isidro Market, Tegucigalpa

There is a bored guard balancing his shotgun on the palm of his hand. No one wants to steal packs of underwear today. Something is grilling, something squawking. Fish in a wheelbarrow. A plane howls in tight maneuvers between the hilltops of the city for a trick approach; the sidewalks are choked with tomatoes and spare parts for blenders; vendors are hanging boxes over the concrete railing of the bridge overlooking a dry riverbed where kids are inventing games to play with broken flip-flops; and I step around dog food in burlap sacks, onions with tops, onions without tops. "Hey, Blanco, take my picture." Everybody needs to run into the catacomb of concrete stalls to allow buses to squeeze through, their destinations yelled like mad bird songs, and the zinc roof sucks away the security of sunlight and traps the scent of pig carcasses. I slip on blood. "Hey, you, look at my potatoes." And past the banana bunch ramparts, I ask myself where does the market

end, does it end? I duck under Spider-Man piñatas—
"Blanco, take my picture"—and I end up on a dirt alley, in
a stall of AMERICAN GOODS, between the Levis and the Con-
verses, a false sense of the familiar in a sea of lost.

The Comb of Rebellion

Three dollars. It can't even get you a beer in a New York City bar. But it's the going rate for a haircut in Panama City. Peppered all over the El Cangrejo neighborhood, the barbershops, too many for the available number of scalps, all advertise the same rate. Then again, I never saw a Panama City dweller with a hair out of place.

When in the capital, I decided that I must have stood out. My cowlicks flared at will, encouraged by the humidity. I was something to gawk at. My four-pocketed guayabera shirt, a standard of the capital, wasn't fooling anyone, so I assigned myself the mission of acquiring said three-dollar cut to complete my disguise.

I didn't have to walk far to find the closest barbershop. I just followed the cheerful neon shouting *abierto*. The inside of the salon, however, sulked in cinderblock drabness. In one corner of the waiting room (or was it a burrow?), a magazine hovered in front of a man's face. A child, probably his son, dragged a toy around on the stubby carpet. Enthusiasm hovered at an ominous low.

Without moving the magazine, the man gestured to me to pick up a catalog that featured nothing but pictures of some of the timeless Central American male hairstyles: neat, greased up, geometric crops fashioned from short bursts of black hair. They were the kind of styles that complement pimped-out slacks and a smooth salsa step. Pity I possessed neither the pimped-out slacks (I traveled light) nor a dance-floor dominance (mostly forgotten).

The man lifted his gaze, revealing a doughy, cratered face slickened with sweat or some kind of anti-pimple ointment. His coffee-bean eyes hid somewhere under his brows. He had the kind of unsettlingly oversized head you'd expect to find on a marble statue, not on someone who will be whizzing blades around your face. In a soft murmur, the dough parted, and he asked me if I was ready.

Even though I couldn't find a fitting cut in his catalog, and even though I felt like a hobbit compared to his jawbone, my desire to support the local economy kept me gazing at the cinderblocks. Maybe he could give me another kind of style? Saying that I wanted a short cut that's a little pointed up at the front—like what one could find at the barber shops in New York City's East Village—wouldn't help. So I gave him a hopelessly vague answer. Could he give me my current style, but shorter?

He didn't respond as he led me down a hall, darker and deeper into the burrow. At the end, his cutting room, free of windows, relied on a dusty fluorescent bulb that colored the countertop a cigarette-filter yellow. Everything was chunky and dull, like communist-era surplus. Why did he have to bring me so far back into the building? Didn't he have to keep watch on his son?

It occurred to me that this secluded corner of the building would be ideal for harvesting someone's wallet and/or organs. I considered telling him that I had changed my mind and didn't fancy a trim after all, that I intended to offer myself as fodder for hustlers and pickpockets.

But isn't one of the benefits of travel to experience the unfamiliar? By that logic, I chose to stay. I decided it would be quite an accomplishment for him to steal a kidney or two using only a pair of scissors and a comb (now *that* would make a hell of a pub story). I just wished I were able to extract an ounce of intent from those secluded eyes of his.

When he held up his comb, I noticed something that was—well, unfamiliar. The comb was covered in a blob of dark hairs, a lush anthology of probably three hundred dollars' worth of past services. In his other hand, the scissors boasted their very own hair-cakes, impossibly thick, like the glue-on mustaches the cops wear in grade-B, teenage horror flicks.

It was possible that I'd end up with more hair stuck to my head than when we started, along with whatever egg-laying critters that might happen to enjoy camping out in pomade and salsa sweat.

Surely, with a chuckle, he'll notice the lapse of hygiene and wipe off his instruments, I said to myself. But he didn't chuckle. Instead, he began approaching, hairy scissors cocked, lunging in a relaxed pace, affording me just enough time to silently gasp.

Now, allow me to interject with a little of my wander-lust philosophy. When I travel, I like to go about life as the locals do. If they slurp up an unnamed meat stew, I hand over my bowl for a helping. If everyone shares luggage-carrying duties on a bus, I fall in line and serve as a communal Sherpa. Perhaps the barber's sanitary economy was normal for the address. Let the ugly Americans be as ugly (and clean) as they want inside their hermetically sealed coach buses.

But at this turn, I broke my own rule. My triple-ply, plastic-bagged American upbringing had temporarily hijacked my travel sense. I violated the prime directive. I asked him to clean the scissors. With an apologetic *por favor*.

He stopped in an unnatural, pained freeze. I finally saw the whites of his eyes. *"Gringos*, damn princes!" grumbled the thought balloon above his stare. Then he disappeared into another room.

I imagined that he might want to thank me for my criticism of his barbering technique by returning with a machete. "Is this blade clean enough?" he'll ask while solving that pesky long hair problem in one swing to the jugular. The things I do to support local economies...

Before I could contemplate either a more drastic apology—or an escape—he returned sans-machete, his eyes reverting back to their normal size and temperature. For my approval, he displayed the pair of scissors, its mustaches completely shaved off. The comb was bald. Nowhere for lice eggs to hunker down, I said to myself more than a few times.

By the way, I should mention that my knowledge of such little insects is based on past brushes (no pun intended) with them in Panama, since head lice are a fact of life in the tropical country, albeit more prevalent in some of the rural areas. In Guna Yala, an autonomous archipelago where the indigenous Guna live in cozy formation on tiny islands, I've seen the Guna lovingly pluck the pests off of each other's heads. Just another afternoon chore.

Such a good deed changed the country forever. Delousing was one of the many activities that the Panamanian police, who occupied the Guna islands until 1925, viewed as uncivilized. The police beat any Guna caught in the act of plucking and tossing. The Guna responded to the colonial choke chain with the Guna Uprising of 1925, which ended up tossing the police off the islands (such a poetic form of delousing) and awarding the Guna with autonomy. So as you can see, humble little lice can be seen as accomplices to a revolution, in an unkempt, punk rock kind of way.

Either that, or I was trying to rationalize the possibility that I'd return to the States with a dozen six-legged, undeclared, duty-free hitchhikers. And I doubt that the stranger sitting next to me in coach on the flight home would indulge me, with tweezers in hand, in bringing that number down some.

The barber was already going at my hair. Mashing his forehead into an oddly channeled concentration, he snipped in slow arcs, as if his mind were only half-focused on the task. And half-focused on what else? What was going on behind those dough-brows?

If I ended up with one of his catalog haircuts, complete with a shellacking of grease, maybe that would be a good thing. Maybe the bloodsucking insects would slip right off my head, riding down my hairs like slides in a kiddie park.

"Is that okay?" he asked me.

I turned in the mirror and stared with a strange, timeless pause. Not only had he succeeded in reverse-engineering my hairstyle, he had given me the best haircut I'd had in years. Even hairstylists in the East Village, with the aid of pictures on the wall, sometimes flub it up at four times the price. All those peculiar glances in mid-snip turned out to be nothing more than the barber peeking at his son in the other room.

My wallet remained in my pocket. All internal organs remained properly connected to one another. And he accomplished the cut without the help of a single louse. I guess I am just not punk rock enough for Panama. I'm a rebel without a parasite. But quite a dapper rebel, I should add.

When I relate the above in person, my listeners tend to back away from me in careful steps. Even though I had unfairly underestimated the sanitary habits of the barber (I think), I still like to add a little flair to the storytelling by giving my head a scratch here or there.

The Mountain Loaves

It began with a nervous laugh. Then a familiar voice: "What are you doing here? You're *dead*."

So went a dream I had over a decade ago. My surroundings seemed real—the walls were solid, the sun glowed just as intensely as always, and my friends and family were talking and gesturing just as I remembered them. I had just noticed that the gathering was some sort of cocktail party when a high school friend, one I hadn't seen since graduation, guided me aside with a gentle, trembling nudge and delivered the above information.

While one is still part of the living, the question of where one ends up after being freed from the mortal tether tends to have as many answers as those who are asked. In front of pearly gates. Under a score of naked, perpetually young attendants who fuss over you. Before a list of all the selfish things you did. Or the place may be more of a state of mind, a product of the lack of oxygen to the brain, precipitating wicked hallucinations that bring visions of unfathomable fantasy.

Or you might end up being a party crasher.

This question burbled in my mind while Melanie and I were hiking up a steep mud path on the mainland coast across from Ukupseni, an island in Panama's Guna Yala archipelago. Along with our young and bony Guna guide, Alicio, we were headed to the village's burial grounds. Unlike most indigenous groups of the Americas, the Guna of Panama's Caribbean coast have resisted domination by Western entities, and thus their customs have remained as intact as they wish them to be. I wondered what the burial site would reveal about the Guna's traditional views of life, afterlife, and spirits.

But we were first treated to a lesson of the living. Alicio had just crouched down next to a highway of leafcutter ants crossing the path. He grabbed the pieces of leaves they were carrying, and then flung off the ants. "These leaves make good medicine," he said, speaking of the Guna's knowledge of botany that has been passed down for centuries. Then he added, "We are too lazy to pick them ourselves." And what kind of affliction will a prepared bath made from the leaves cure? "Laziness."

I hadn't expected such lightheartedness as we arrived at his community's cemetery, which followed an irregular swath of packed dirt on a plateau about a hundred feet above the coast. The village buried their deceased under mounds of dirt that reminded me of loaves of bread rising from baking pans.

But such prime real estate attracts competition. If the deceased was a hunter, Alicio explained, the jawbones of the game he had claimed were strung above his grave to protect it against any evil spirits that have a knack for mountain climbing.

One loaf had been staked with a concrete cross. Alicio followed my line of sight and said, "We don't encourage that kind of burial." Despite the independent mindset of the Guna, Christianity's tantalizing promise of total absolution has still managed to sneak in. Since I counted just one cross, it appeared that Jesus had only managed to secure a modest spiritual beachhead into the community of Ukupseni.

I wished to take a cue from the other mourners as to the protocol of the afternoon, so that I would not disrespect anyone, it being my first visit to a Guna burial site. I stayed quiet and kept my head lowered, because I figured that's what one does during a cemetery visit, at least from my experience in cemeteries in America. The mourners stop by, pray solemnly, place flowers or another memento near the tombstone, and leave, as if the cemetery were a mountaintop inhospitable to humans save for brief visits.

But none of that drill applied to the Guna burial site. Instead, while swaying gently on a hammock swung between the poles above her mother's remains, a woman was sewing a *mola*, a colorful work of embroidery that she'll either sew onto her own clothes or sell to a tourist. Each family brought a bag with a picnic snack. Chatting tickled the breeze. Not a tear streamed down the mounds. The Guna outing seemed to be more of a warm celebration of life, as if the gathered were visiting an old relative.

I spun around. I looked up past the occasional cashew apple lying on the ground, and set my eyes over the magnificent vista of the island of Ukupseni and the nearby islands and reefs, surrounded by the deep blueness of the

Caribbean that melted into the horizon. It was then that I began to appreciate why the Guna chose such a place to bury their dead. To afford the spirits such an unequalled panorama is to afford them with perpetual dignity and respect.

One of the greatest feelings when traveling is making an unexpected connection, an understanding that can, if just for a moment, open up one culture to another. I turned to Alicio and said, "For the Guna, the dead have the best view."

He crumpled his brows. "No they don't," he said. "They're *dead*."

Subdued by Street Vendors

"Chicken, chicken, soda, soda!"

I was sweating in a parked bus, serenaded by barks from Managua's version of curb service. I didn't believe the vendors would be able to stand tall enough to push their products through the high safety windows of the bus, a reincarnated Blue Bird that used to haul American kids to school. But greasy plates tilted their way in, as if I were sitting in the innards of a giant row of slot machines.

Not to feel left out, I shouted out an order just before the bus left the terminal. With help from a vendor's beanstalk arms, I received not-so-recently fried chicken, more bone than meat, and a plastic bag of Coca Cola. My gringo hands allowed me to slurp out about a nickel's worth of Coke before I dropped the squishy thing during the jolts of the geriatric engine. Thus my culinary exploration of Matagalpa, the mild-aired mountain city in the belly button of

Nicaragua's coffee country—our destination—prematurely began.

As my sneaker treads stuck to corn syrup, I wondered how the Matagalpa area, rich in crops and livestock, had rebounded from the abuse of the Contra War during the 1980s. But you wouldn't know that Matagalpa survived some of the nastier guerilla fighting of the conflict if you glanced at the cheerful folks on the bus en route to the city. Hemorrhaging distorted classic rock through speakers mounted on the ceiling, the bus turned into a carnival when a tiny bird made the mistake of flying into an open window. In a country with more than its share of comically rabid baseball players, I knew the bird wouldn't last long before being caught by a pair of bare hands. After being gently tossed out the window, the bird found itself free again,

I would soon discover from where Nicaraguan short-stops had inherited their coordination. When the bus spilled us onto the tight sidewalks of Matagalpa, I had to duck around a procession of women balancing wooden trays of oranges on their heads. They swung both arms at their sides without a crumple of concentration. Smooth and unhurried, their steps ended up creating an odd elegance, as if the women were flaunting peculiar hats topped with fruit patterns.

Matagalpa inhales and exhales food. It's a playground for provisions. Such a reality seems contradictory in light of the country's economy having been ravaged by wars, hurricanes, and presidents pocketing international relief money. Yet none of those gruesome setbacks prevent farmers from bringing down produce from the surrounding mountainsides and making a living.

With the city's avocado stands and stew carts and head-balanced produce blocking pedestrians, I realized I wouldn't need to walk inside a restaurant to eat. Or maybe that was their plan. How else could I explain a vendor setting up a grill on a sidewalk so narrow she makes pedestrians walk in a sluggish single line past her cart, forcing them to snort up sweet puffs of grilling banana leaves and corn tortillas? I was helpless. Like flies stuck in a web, pedestrians became ensnared in banana leaf smoke and found themselves ordering 9-córdoba (50¢) *guirilas*, thick tortillas wrapped in said leaves and stuffed with fresh *cuajada* cheese.

The streets of Matagalpa were about to get more crowded, thanks to a truly Nicaraguan brand of Catholicism. Across from the city's central supermarket, a deejay's boxing-arena announcements shot from speakers aboard a truck trailer painted with advertising for a canned tuna company. The trailer had no walls, all the better to watch three caramel-colored young ladies grinding hot pants and spinning miniskirts to the beat of the company's jingle. "La Sirena tuna is the richest," screamed the tweeters, as the girls shook their spandex-slung, sun-ripened produce for the approval of a crowd collecting on the sidewalk. Holy Week and Easter were approaching in a few weeks, and the city decided that the best way to butter up God was with lent-friendly offerings of hot pants (no meat, right?) and spiced fish in a can.

The trailer kept bouncing up and down more than a mattress in a love hotel. People emerged from the store with armfuls of the chili flavor. Shaky pyramids of the lemon flavor. Oranges scattered as fruit stands tipped over, smacked by the spasmodic knees of men trying to get a better look at what exactly makes La Sirena the richest. And that is how tuna is sold in Nicaragua.

IN NICARAGUAN STREET TAKE-OUT, cups and bottles are viewed as strange extravagances because everyone sips their on-the-go beverages out of plastic bags. The factory-sealed varieties resemble melted ice packs the little league coach would toss at a kid after he slid into second base all wrong. But unlike the home-poured sandwich bag of Coca Cola I fumbled in the bus, the factory-made bags don't come with a straw. When confronted with such a quandary, the Nica drinker bites a hole in the corner and squeezes the bag while cradling it, like suckling on a boob.

The burbling breakfast pots along the edges of Parque Morazán, adjacent to the city's inescapably gigantic cathedral, provided me with rice, beans, and roast chicken, all of which I washed down with a bag of *chicha de maiz*, a corn drink. A little fermented, a little sweetened, and unsettlingly pulpy, the bright purple juice matched the jovial paintjobs and neocolonial architecture of the buildings, so much that I almost forgot that most of the city was constructed out of concrete.

The city's brightness and bustle have also obscured the effects of the recent war, aside from the city's monument for the tomb of the unknown Sandinista soldier and a few veterans hopping around on crutches in the parks. When I met Rafael, a middle-aged science fiction author, I was going to ask him how Matagalpa survived the war so well. Rafael, like many Nicas, had left the country during the

Contra War and didn't return until the Contras disbanded. So instead, he and I ended up debating whether recent teleportation experiments in physics actually moved particles themselves, or merely information about the particles. It was a conversation I hadn't anticipated having while drinking corn beer out of a plastic bag.

Snacks call for an equally simple container: the napkin sheath...unless you're a superhero. When Spider-Man visits Nicaragua, he must be bored without the Green Goblin around, so he stays sharp by snagging hotdogs with his web-shooter. Or at least that's what the hand-painted artwork on the side of the park's pushcart vendor depicts.

I OFTEN WONDER if Nicaraguans laugh at Americans who cultivate chia pets, but not because of the pets' campy, stuttering jingle on late-night commercials. When an American grows a chia pet's hair only to chuck the sprouts after a few weeks, a Nica would view the practice as a waste of tasty food. Since chia (also spelled chilla) is native to Central America, the many cultures that have lived there during the past few millennia—including the Maya—have been eating the sprouts as well as the seeds.

Don Chaco's restaurant, Matagalpa's epicenter of natural shakes, mixed the seeds in a tall glass with lemon juice and sugar to make their tangy drink *chilla con limon*, Nicaragua's answer to Taiwan's bubble tea. The seeds, when wet, form little gelatinous spheres around themselves, and when I sucked them up through a straw, they gave me the same exciting sensation of not knowing whether I've just sucked up a tapioca ball or a fly.

I ALWAYS SEEM TO ATTRACT drunks in my travels. Maybe I've listened to too many Tom Waits songs. Maybe it's my appreciation of hearing thoughts stripped down to their candid essentials by a buoyant blood alcohol level. Or, in the case of yet another encounter on a narrow Matagalpan side street, two construction workers invited me to chat with their easy-to-understand, boozy Spanish. They had finished their shifts and were now hard at work on a bottle of Caballito, or "Little Horse," the country's White Castle of hooch. Any rural road in Nicaragua would be naked without a few crushed and faded plastic Caballito bottles underfoot.

But drowning in sorrows they were not. "Tell me, amigo, what country has the best beaches, mountains, lakes, seafood, volcanoes, landscapes, and gold?" one asked me. He didn't wait for me to answer. "It's Nicaragua!" he gloated without a hint of irony. His friend nodded in agreement after a slight post-Caballito grimace and passed the bottle.

I reflected on how I had been struck by the attractiveness of vistas almost everywhere I looked in the country (excepting the sprawling chaos of Managua). I'm sure the views helped, but happiness is a frame of mind, after all. How the duo can have so little yet still trumpet their country, the second poorest in the Western hemisphere, showed a resilient coping mechanism and an intrepid lust for life that's AWOL in the world of cubicles and plasma televisions and Hello Kitty waffle makers.

※

AT 4 AM, the cathedral must have been locked because I awoke to a throng of people mumbling prayers of mass in the street. A warped brass band, filling in the silences with soggy, funeral-like blurts, provided accompaniment. It was another Holy Week preparation. But without bikini tops and tuna, just what did they think they were doing?

After their performance, I could not fall back asleep, so at sunrise, I walked to the Parque Morazán. Far from chocolate, the bag of *chicha de cacao*, or cacao juice, I bought from a breakfast vendor on the sidewalk was white and tasted like coconut because the seeds were not dried and fermented. The juice packed plenty of energy for my imminent hike around a coffee cooperative in nearby La Reina.

Abandoned by cronies of the Somoza family (the American-backed dictators that ran the country for four decades until overthrown by the Sandinistas in 1979), the Danilo Gonzalez cooperative resulted from the Sandinistas' redistribution of oligarchic land to *campesinos* (farmers). The cooperative, founded in 1983, sells Fair Trade coffee, guaranteeing members $1.35 per pound of Arabica beans, about double what they would receive from a traditional middleman. The latter offer is often not enough for farmers to break even.

During the Contra War, brigades of European volunteers arrived to pick coffee beans on this farm to keep the Nicaraguan wartime economy going, an effort that failed because the brigades competed with the Contras, who were destroying crops, schools, and ports. Both sides heavily mined the countryside in the 1980s, a fact I considered when the guide led me into the lushness of the farm's coffee bushes, although the Matagalpa area has been mine-free since 2002. Farmers who could not wait for the under-funded de-mining teams taught themselves clearing techniques, and thus mines became one of Nicaragua's lesser-known bumper crops.

After facing a burden of over 170,000 mines in her soil, Nicaragua has claimed that at the current rate of mine removal, the country will be declared free of the weapons in just a few years. While that's a statistic to be proud of, I would bet the tourism board is having a difficult time capitalizing on it. Come to Nicaragua: almost all the mines have been cleared!

The project is helping fifty-three farmers make a living in a country that is half unemployed or underemployed. With such a success story, the farm could make a killing on tourists if the farm built a tasting room and sold coffee bags. But the tourism aspect of the farm is still young, and for now, the farm representatives told me to buy Matagalpan Fair Trade coffee when I'm in the States, since that keeps the whole Fair Trade system going.

With my cheeks full of rum-flavored chocolates made by hand at the nearby Castillo del Cacao (Chocolate Castle), I climbed into the bus that would take me back to the capital. Vendors entered with baskets of water boobs and *rosquillas*—buttery cheese cookies. Bustle as usual. I realized that in Matagalpa, the people did not allow their war-torn past to hold the present hostage. I never discovered where the aggression went.

I was left wondering about other Nicaraguan conundrums, like why the so-called express bus was making a stop on the highway. We pulled into a lot that looked like an abandoned bus terminal and the driver shut off the engine.

Then the shouting began. From the outside.

Approaching the bus from every direction, arcs of white teeth aimed upward, open mouths hollering in a vicious drone. There were too many of them. I couldn't make out what they were saying. Did they have someone's head on a stick? Did they want someone's head on a stick?

I tried to discern whether the mob was robbing the bus, but I had to make that decision quickly because they were beginning to reach up into the windows, trying to shove in dark objects that wouldn't fit.

And then I began to understand the shouts. We were being invaded by bags of onions and half-green tomatoes.

Once the front door was breached, in came the squadrons of ice cream vendors. Then a wave of mushy fried chicken, apparently cooked during Reagan's first term. They strafed us with rosquillas, the vendors pushing free samples towards our mouths. Okay! I surrender! I'll eat it!

I seemed to have discovered a new generation of Nicaraguan guerilla maneuvers after all. To defend yourself, instead of needing an AK-47, you need to draw out your haggling skills and a quick sense of what produce is the ripest. And you might want to keep some charcoal tablets in your holster in case you need to reckon with that fried chicken.

Pop-Up Nicaragua

Maybe it was the late afternoon sun glazing the pastel-colored walls that did it. Or maybe it was the smell of horse crap. As I sat in Granada's Parque Central, I ignored the covers of guidebooks flapping around me, and I imagined I was sitting in the park in the mid-nineteenth century.

That's impressive irony, since most of the city's buildings are less than 125 years old. Granada, Nicaragua burned to the ground in 1857, thanks to the adventures of an American that few Americans have ever heard about. Stateside schoolbooks rarely, if at all, mention the exploits of Tennessee-born privateer William Walker, the sixth president of the Republic of Nicaragua.

If the above sentences sound like lead lines from a work of historical fiction, then you should keep in mind the zeitgeist of America in the mid-nineteenth century, dominated by two words: Manifest Destiny. In other words, we Americans are ravenous, wealthy, armed, and we're on a winning streak, so everything on this continent, drawn in those maps with overly ornate compasses, is ordained to be ours.

It was a time when you didn't need cockamamie pretenses to invade countries. You just went in. Like when America invaded Mexico in 1846 and ingested half her territory. (As economist and native rights activist Winona LaDuke likes to point out, the word "colonize" comes from the same root as "colon.") But for William Walker, that wasn't enough. Standing a quaint five foot three but full of white supremacy, Walker rounded up a few dozen bandits and briefly occupied two of the remaining Mexican states, Baja California and Sonora, in 1853. He put the region under the laws of Louisiana, a slave state, until Mexican resistance forced Walker to retreat to the States.

His thirst for conquest unslaked by his outing in Mexico, Walker headed for Nicaragua in 1855. At that time, Nicaragua was in the middle of a civil war, a fact not lost on Walker. He employed a standard tactic used by many a conqueror: choose a place with a civil conflict and nuzzle up to a side; that way, half the country is already on your team. He not only captured the capital and set up a puppet government, he also began recruiting mercenaries to attack other Central American countries for future U.S. slave states.

Emboldened by his initial success, he proclaimed himself president of Nicaragua in 1856. He declared English as the official language of Nicaragua and reinstituted slavery of blacks and Native Americans. In the process, he helped unite a divided Nicaragua—against *him*, that is. As a result, brigades from several Central American countries routed Walker's troops to a pasty pulp. The United States navy then hastened a rescue of this Napoleon-sized Caligula-of-the-tropics.

Walker torched Granada just before he escaped. He was greeted in New York as a hero. The next year, when he attempted to invade Central America again, his welcoming party in Honduras captured him and delivered him to an eager firing squad.

There's no point in mentioning a three-time loser in American schoolbooks, is there? If you want to know more about Walker, don't fret—you can always ask a Nicaraguan.

As if to spite Walker's romp, Granada not only rebuilt itself, it also utilized the same colonial style of architecture. Several cathedrals survived, albeit with still-visible scorch marks. The largest cathedral, facing Parque Central, was finished in 1915 but appears as if it followed 300-year-old blueprints.

Modern-day Granada appears so much like the Granada into which Walker victoriously marched that director Alex Cox shot footage for *Walker*, his 1987 movie about said conqueror, in the same narrow streets in which I was roaming. But he didn't aim to create a period piece; Cox, who directed the film during the Contra War (in which the CIA supported the Contra side), weaved shards of the 1980s into his movie: thugs reading *Time* magazine on stage coaches, a stray military helicopter dropping from the sky. Cox's blurring of the timeline reminds us that American intervention in Nicaragua has an often repetitive history.

I stopped in front of a snow cone cart parked in front of the cathedral. Painted with poses of Spider-Man, the cart, framed by towering mustard-yellow steeples behind it, seemed like one of Cox's glaring anachronisms. I half-expected Ollie North to appear and offer to buy me a double.

Today, troops have given way to tourists. Neo-hippies selling jewelry. Circles of backpackers camouflaged in soiled, faded clothing of the same shade—backpacker brown. DSLR barrels dangling from necks like ripe avocados.

But many Americans were not in town to get pictures of themselves standing in front of the towering cathedral. Hotel breakfast rooms reverberated with the chatter of MacBook-toting gringos discussing real estate transactions and title questions. "Now that the bad Sandinista years are long gone," I overheard an investor boasting, "it's a great time to build luxury hotels in Nicaragua." When I asked one sun-reddened American buyer, who planned on retiring in Nicaragua, what he thought of the country's real estate climate, he answered, "Everything is for sale!" I realized that I had stepped into the latest wave of American involvement in Nicaragua.

How was Granada taking this incursion? Will foreign ownership of larger amounts of land change the soul of the country? At least for the vendors in the park, the flow of visitors has created a roaring business. If I stopped moving, vendors laden with hammocks and jewelry swooped upon my flesh faster than gnats. When a shoeshine boy failed to score a shine from me (a messy shoe paintjob was closer to what he was offering), he tried to sell me his folded-up homework instead.

I walked westward, past the Internet cafes and fusion restaurants serving lentil burgers, down side streets patrolled by women with bundles of brooms balanced on their heads. MUERTE A LOS TICOS (Death to the Costa

Ricans) declared graffiti scrawled on a quiet corner building, referring to a rift between Nicaraguan farmhands working in Costa Rica and the host Costa Ricans. The latter claim the Nicaraguans are taking jobs away from Costa Ricans, albeit the manual labor jobs are the ones that few Costa Ricans care to take. In a nearby restaurant with heinously yellow fluorescent lights splashing on plastic chairs, a poster taped to the wall contained a map of Nicaragua, stating Nicaragua's territorial dispute with Colombia over a few islands in the Caribbean, stemming back to a U.S.-backed deal in Colombia's favor signed "at gunpoint." The English-language din I had heard around the Parque Central had died several blocks ago. If everything in Nicaragua was for sale, this restaurant would probably be one of the holdouts.

"MOST OF THE HOUSES on the islands are owned by local families," shouted Pedro, my boatman, over the rumble of the outboard engine. He was taking me around Las Isletas, a cluster of islands in Lake Nicaragua near Granada. "But this one," he said while gesturing to a half-built, multi-level structure, "is going to be a hotel."

Despite docking at an island restaurant in the center of Las Isletas, a dreamy archipelago filled with turtles sunning themselves in front of vistas of conical volcanoes, the restaurant still sold cheap beers unaffected by the presence of prospectors on the mainland. Amidst the Spanish-language chatter, I noticed that the families having drinks at the restaurant were from Granada, and several knew Pedro.

I wondered if mothers would still be shampooing heads of toddlers at the side of the lake in ten years. Did the gentle waves that day resemble a calmness before a storm of gentrified anguish? Or would outside investment deliver income to the working people of the second-poorest country in the Western Hemisphere? I had seen what an acute income divide brought on by absentee owners had done to areas in neighboring Costa Rica, leading to resentment and inevitable crime.

Back in Parque Central, I held up a t-shirt from a vendor's table. T-shirts, the chief stylistic export of comfort-forward American fashion, are usually—perhaps appropriately—emblazoned with English words, no matter where they are sold. The one I selected, however, contained a famous quotation, in Spanish, from Augusto Sandino, the Nicaraguan leader of guerilla forces who, in the late 1920s and early 1930s, opposed the occupation of the country by the U.S. Marines. "If there are just one hundred men who love Nicaragua the way I do, then Nicaragua will be free," declared the shirt along with a silk-screened image of him in his distinctively oversized cowboy hat. He and his men, who fought with both gruesomeness and passion, hid in the mountains so well that the marines never captured them. But after the marines ended their occupation, the U.S.-supported leader of Nicaragua's National Guard assassinated him, elevating Sandino to martyr.

The vendor glanced at me with an odd mixture of pride and curiosity, as if to ask, "Why is a gringo buying that shirt?" When I explained I knew who Sandino was, his eyes became giant and happy and he said, "There is no equal."

With the rush of tourists and foreign money, Nicaragua finds itself at a precarious crossroads. I hesitate to guess what path she will follow. Instead, I shall leave you with a pungent suggestion of the country's brand of resilience, in the form of a sign I found hanging outside a funeral home. The hand-painted image portrayed an open coffin, its tuxedo-wearing occupant popping up, arms out. He wore the grin of a party animal. Like the roughly drawn but cheerful fellow, Nicaragua has a tendency to pop back up again, no matter what others may try to do.

Rock Hotel Hospitality

Just before sunrise on September 4, 2007, lobster divers in Nicaragua's Miskito Cays awoke to the ghoulish sounds of roof thatch shredding apart. The floor planks of their over-the-water camps flew off the posts before they could pray. The night before, several groups of fishermen had deemed the warnings of an approaching hurricane a false alarm, one of many false alarms over past years.

Hurricane Felix made sure his arrival was not misunderstood. With 160-mile-per-hour winds, Felix destroyed every house on the Cays and nine thousand more on the Nicaraguan mainland, and killed over one hundred people, dozens of them lobster divers. But as I would discover, nature was not the divers' most difficult adversary.

HAND-PAINTED ADVERTISEMENTS lend themselves a certain longevity. They exude a one-of-a-kind craftsmanship, either intentionally or not, that almost negates the sign's commercial nature, an effect absent from the act of tacking up a perfect, pre-printed billboard, which can be un-tacked in another instant.

Five months after a direct hit from Felix, a hand-painted ad for a hardware store took on a new sense of longevity as it remained near the four-hundred-foot mark on the wall of the baseball diamond of Bilwi, the mainland port across from the Miskito Cays. The bleachers' roof had been torn off. When I arrived, Bilwi was rebuilding itself, one roof panel at a time.

I wasn't sure in what condition I would find Bilwi because a few weeks after Felix brought its fury over northwestern Nicaragua, news sources dropped their coverage and rushed on to the next excitingly fresh world disaster. A fifty-cent cab ride from the airport parted the town's thick air, a humid breath of Caribbean casualness, and revealed that the town's center had been, for the most part, spared. The block-sized Central Park, surrounded by stocky concrete structures, had lost its trees but still attracted young lovers and daytime drunks. By the time I arrived, most of the corrugated zinc roofs had been repaired and had already started to rust from the coast's hit-and-run rainstorms. Looking toward the shoreline, I saw that many palm trees still lined the bluff overlooking the town's beach. And restaurants had begun serving lobster tails again.

Sure, I'd come to a place where I could indulge in a $7 plate of said shellfish, but I had also come so I could understand the isolated port's relationship with the precious crustacean.

But first, I needed to pick up the rhythm of the trilingual port itself. I began absorbing the mélange of Miskito, English, and Spanish chatter in the concrete-tiled roads. The occasional army truck loaded with Nicaraguan soldiers cruised by, as if to remind the town that Managua, a sprawling city on the other side of the country, is the capital. It seems the folks of Bilwi, the most populated center of the Miskito Coast, would rather not listen. The native Miskito nation, who make up almost half the population of Bilwi, have been battling invaders for centuries, and owing to their history of clever trading and fierce fighting, have never been thoroughly subjugated.

The Miskito even survived the conquistadors' free-for-all of the sixteenth and seventeenth centuries. The British, in an odd departure from colonial behavior, didn't bother with slaughtering the Miskito, and instead became their trading partners, the two allies fighting against the Spaniards together. Such exposure to Western culture, especially when the British traded them guns, helped the Miskito become a regional power, during which time many Miskito traders learned English. Their influence in the southern Caribbean became so widespread that the waters from Nicaragua to Panama were labeled MOSQUITO (sic) BAY on an 1862 map.

The Miskito have maintained their language, despite Bilwi having been renamed Puerto Cabezas after General Rigoberto Cabezas, who invaded the Miskito Coast in 1894, annexing the territory for Nicaragua. Since then, the Miskito have not had full control over their own land. But when the image of the lobster went from garbage to gourmet a few decades ago, lobstering provided the most lucrative work for the Miskito.

The homemade wooden wheelchairs being cranked around the roads gave me an indication that the work came at an irreversible cost. When most of the lobsters from shallow water were taken, the divers strapped on scuba gear and dove deeper to find them. Due to faulty equipment and poor training, the divers rose to the surface too fast and too often, giving themselves the decompression illness known as the bends, leaving many paralyzed or with heinous neurological damage. Most current lobstermen have learned how to dive safely, but some still push the limits of physiology because the more cholesterol-heavy critters they can snag in a day, the more cash they score. A caustic cocktail of poverty, unawareness, and greed—greed on the part of the boat captains, importers/exporters, and some of the divers themselves—has proven to be more detrimental to the divers' lives than a hurricane.

Considering such a burden of adversity, I wanted to support the Miskito economy, and the best place to start was the town's Miskito Market, which winds through the center of town through unnamed streets and alleys. A scattering of zinc panels overhead offered a respite from the sun but also gave the market an uneasy, cavernous feel, contrasting with the humbling vastness of the Caribbean Sea just a few hundred meters away. Kiosks made of faded tropical hardwoods hawked t-shirts, toy slingshots ("They're good for shutting up roosters," the vendor told me), and used shoes. Plates, cups, pirated video games. Every creature comfort for your wood-slab house. Thanks to my airline losing my luggage, I was on the lookout for new clothing, and through the countless kiosks selling seemingly enough attire to outfit the entire coast, I could not find one pair of socks large enough to fit my bony gringo feet.

A few steps from the clothing stalls, the market began to sell food and meat. Baskets of gnarled root vegetables called *badu*. Burlap bags of beans. Obscenely juicy tomatoes. I stepped over barbecue pits on ground, burned out from the previous evening, to find branches of the market sprouting off the main grotto—or maybe each branch was an entrance to someone's backyard.

I found daylight again and returned to the roads, eager to test out my slingshot on unsuspecting poultry and to squeeze my feet into the tiny booties that pass for socks on the Miskito Coast. A few girls sitting in front of a church sold me a plastic bag of *arroz con piña*, a rice with pineapple drink, which I sipped by biting a hole in the bag and squeezing its contents into my mouth, a trick I'd seen the locals accomplish less messily than I had. Finding a curbside garbage pail in Bilwi in which to deposit the bag was challenging because there aren't any. Rather, the side of the road is the communal garbage pail from which chickens and stray dogs scrounge their lunches. As for the bags, they just blow around and fade a little, tangling themselves in trees, Nicaragua's urban tumbleweeds.

Such an adventure in sanitation seems less surprising in a town where a bridge overlooking a dump doubled as a hangout, where I saw a few kids watching iguanas and dinosaur-skinned buzzards picking through cow skulls and bags of rotting tomatoes below. What the beasts don't eat gets burned, and the fumes embedded themselves in my clothes for days.

The air was fresher out on the end of Bilwi's kilometer-long dock, known as El Muelle. The dock used to stretch farther into the Caribbean Sea in the middle of the twentieth century, when it first served Bilwi's lumber rush, and then as a launching point for naval ships during the CIA-engineered invasion of Cuba's Bay of Pigs in 1961. Since then, the last quarter of it has collapsed, claimed plank by plank, by storms and voracious saltwater, as if to atone for its role in the failed invasion.

I passed several docked forty-foot vessels on whose hulls rust and algae battled each other. These were lobster boats, discernible by the racks of scuba tanks and stacks of wafer-thin canoes on deck. I must have missed the day's departing divers, for there were none on El Muelle at that moment.

I did, however, meet a few Creole fishermen who dangled their limbs off the jagged planks at the extreme end of the dock. One had just pulled his hook out of an eel-like fish he had reeled in. The dock was in better condition closer to shore, so why brave the gaps in the boards this far out? "It's peaceful out here," one answered. "Yesterday there were seventy boats docked. But they don't dock on this part." Indeed, no one was bothering them except me.

I SUPPOSE SCARFING DOWN a spiny lobster tail dinner is both the best and worst way to help the divers. What benefits them more, supporting their dangerous work or steering them away from it? Despite the divers' predicament, scrapping the lobstering industry has been deemed impractical because so many Miskito rely upon the income. There is always talk of traps replacing scuba tanks, but then there are objections that the traps will destroy the reef. Fishing off the dock instead, a much safer option and, as I'd seen, a relaxing pastime, would not pay a family's expenses.

The neighborhood chickens helped me make my mind up. After taking note of their curiously flexible diet from the roadside buffets, I passed on the wing and thigh platter. At one of Bilwi's open-air restaurants, I ordered spiny lobster ($7 for two tails) and chose the traditional preparation of the area: breaded and fried.

Deep-frying a lobster tail? I can hear the shrieks of the foodies now. "Sacrilege! How dare they destroy a luxury ingredient as if it were bar food! I'll bet those heathens wash it down with *beer!*" Considering the tails' spicy breading, I wondered why anyone would want to dip the tails in a boring cup of butter (as I sipped from a bottle of beer). Better yet was the warm feeling that at $7, even locals can splurge on a lobster meal now and then.

ON THE WALK to a grocery kiosk, I was intercepted by two Miskito carpenters enjoying their day off. They had been shouting their favorite terms of endearment to passing girls while double-teaming a bottle of ninety-cent rum. "We Miskitos like Americans and the British. They helped us," said one, Jeronimo, his pink eyeballs topping a comfortable grin. The other carried an English-language statistics textbook and stared strangely at his grip on the book's spine, then at me. "He loves the English language," Jeronimo told me. "That's why he carries the book with him."

Stat Man, in a wobbly mix of Spanish and English, insisted that I—a surprise ambassador of the English-speaking world—browse his book. He could not read it but he sure knew how to hold it. The cover's veneer of unsavory grime betrayed many an hour of devoted clutching.

Before I could open the cover, Jeronimo crouched down and scratched an outline of Nicaragua in the sand with his finger. He slashed a line down the middle of the country. "This is us," he said, pointing to the northeastern part, "and the other side is Latino." He used the word Latino in the way I've heard many traditional Amerindians use the term, to refer not to themselves, but to Latin Americans of Spanish (or Spanish-Amerindian) descent and Amerindians who have forgotten their culture.

"The Sandinistas are Latinos. We don't trust Sandinistas," Jeronimo said, his smile creases undone. He was referring to the socialists who deposed Nicaragua's last dictator in 1979. During the Contra War, the Sandinistas arrived on the Caribbean coast and began making grand promises of new hospitals and schools that they could not keep, and thus failed to sell their revolution's ideology to the Miskito. Many of the latter were recruited by the CIA-backed Contras instead.

"The British helped us long ago, and then the Americans helped us fight the Sandinistas," Jeronimo said. I felt it was a bad time to mention that the Americans, in 1894, supported Nicaragua's annexation of the Miskito Coast.

After flipping through pages of mathematical derivations and nodding in approval (and hoping I wouldn't be asked what the equations meant), I tried to pass the book back to its owner. "The word Miskito comes from the Spanish word *mixto* (mixed)," Stat Man added in Spanish, leaning into me without grabbing the book. The cover was starting to stick to my hand.

"Yes, mixed!" Jeronimo declared. He broke from the lesson to send out bilingual compliments—in Miskito and Spanish—to a duo of young women walking by. Unfazed by the girls' silence, he bounced his pink eyes back at me. "The Miskito have British and American ancestors. And you are American. You and I are brothers!" He celebrated the apparent family reunion with a slosh of rum from the plastic bottle, which was sold in a handy size that fits in one's pocket. I managed to pass the book back to Stat Man as he started repeating the history of the Miskito Coast, but not before Jeronimo insisted he wanted to name his child after me.

"NO WATER" was the refrain I heard from vendor after vendor. Beer and soda and ninety-cent bottles of rum abounded on the shelves of faded wooden kiosks, but I discovered that in Bilwi, bottled water was almost as hard to find as garbage pails. I settled for mangoes whose sweet juice I would suck out.

The meaty mass of noontime heat slowed the movement of the day. Open doorways of pole houses framed leisurely midday delousings. The Nicaraguan military truck stopped passing by, the soldiers perhaps on siesta. While walking by a fenced-in house, I heard someone calling to me in North American English. Cody, whose yard I was walking past, was scaling fish as he introduced himself and waved me into his concrete dwelling. He showed me his workshop where he employs paralyzed Miskito divers in the construction of solar panels. Along the wheelchair-accessible table, loose pieces of solar panels awaited assembly. The handsome, twenty-something expat, fluent in the Coast's slushy Spanish (along with an expanding Miskito vocabulary), explained that when one in a series of panels fails testing in the factory in the States, the whole series is rejected, but most of it is still usable with some assembly work, so he imports the rejects at a bargain price. Dozens of completed sheets on roofs around town were already drinking up Bilwi's limitless sun.

No assemblers were working that day, so when I mentioned that I was interested in talking with Miskito divers, he offered to take me to a few of their bar hangouts. But that wouldn't be until later on. His arms dotted with fish scales, he invited me to come back for dinner. But what to make? We decided to allow the day's offerings at the Miskito market to choose for us.

With his manual washboard and backyard chickens (that only graze inside his enclosed yard), Cody had adapted to the lifestyle of the town. And that experience extended to the culinary offerings of Bilwi. He knew his way around the market's maze, ushering me to his favorite shrimp vendor. Passing a wheelbarrow full of sea turtle innards, we ducked into an alleyway that opened up into a covered meat market half the size of a basketball court. Fly-covered pig heads bled into a lattice of tabletop machete gashes. Lined up and facing the vendors, buzzards stared rudely from a courtyard next to the market.

After purchasing shrimp from a vendor whose freezer was powered by electricity from who knows where, a nylon net of irritated mud turtles blocked our path. These three-pound staples of the Miskito diet do not boast the international popularity of spiny lobsters, and thus remain free of globalized pressures. No hazardous decompression is required to catch the turtles since they live in shallow rivers. In other words, they're a refreshing alternative in helping to sustain the Miskito economy.

Turtle even finds itself on the menu across the mountains in Latino country. In his 1987 book *The Jaguar Smile: A Nicaraguan Journey*, Salman Rushdie wrote that Nicaraguan president Daniel Ortega served his guests, including Rushdie, a dinner including turtle meat, which Rushdie described as "unexpectedly dense and rich, like a cross between beef and venison."

I felt I should sample such a Nicaraguan mainstay fit for a president...but how does one choose the right turtle? Unfamiliar with the subtleties of picking the best specimen, I used the standard method for selecting a live animal at the market. "I'll take a lively one, please," I said to the vendor.

Cody negotiated to have the vendors prepare the turtle for us. "Quick, get your camera," he said. "These ladies are professionals." By the time the vendor—a humorless woman with whom you would think twice about haggling—had placed the turtle on the hardwood table, several peeking children and aproned vendors gathered around her. But the vendor's work was done. She exchanged places with a younger Miskito woman wearing a couple of gold rings, a long skirt stylish enough for a nightclub, and a calculating smirk. Why had this pillar of confident beauty arrived? Like a perfectly drawn comic book hero (or villain?), she raised a machete. She was The Dispatcher.

She grabbed the turtle by its back legs, waiting for its head to come out. The children watched on with unbroken curiosity—one was sucking on a lollypop—and if they could handle watching her talent, so could I. Besides, The Dispatcher would not wait for the wimps in the crowd to acclimate, nor would she wait for me to compose the perfect picture.

A thwacking sound shot across the market. The Dispatcher's lips stretched into a self-satisfied grin. Another gash for the tabletop lattice.

But she wasn't finished yet. At this point, the onlookers knew to step well back. All except me. Only when shards of shell began flying from the table did I figure out why I should have retreated. The Dispatcher, squeezing her face into a fierce grimace, chipped away at the side of the shell with the machete, throwing off a repetitive chinking sound reminiscent of a low-budget swashbuckling movie. She almost drowned out a man, standing to my side, whom I had just noticed was narrating something into my ear about his welcoming of the Contras' arrival two decades ago.

"THIS PLACE IS DEAD," Cody said as we strolled to the entrance of El Muelle after dark. He was referring to the kiosks, painted with signs declaring WE BUY LOBSTER, lining the road to the dock. Most of them were closed. Since the hurricane, the lobster industry hadn't yet bounced back. In the soupy darkness of the dock entrance, I almost tripped over four sea turtles, three hundred pounds apiece, on their backs, flippers tied up, and still alive. "You won't be seeing *that* for much longer," Cody commented.

The green turtle is endangered, but environmental laws don't have many teeth in northeastern Nicaragua. Nonetheless, the Miskito are well aware of shrinking catches, and they may soon have to forego their traditional meal of sea turtle meat. The Miskitos also know that they have somewhat contributed to the population drop, because for centuries, the Miskito also caught turtles to trade with sailors and pirates. The sea turtles, a godsend for ships of yester-year, kept crews alive on long voyages because after flipping over the turtle and placing it in a cargo hold, it would stay alive for months.

Cody led me back up the dock road to where a pickup truck carrying four teenagers, full of adolescent testosterone and alcohol-spiked blood, stopped in front of us, looking for a confrontation to energize their drifting night. We didn't bite. We stopped the next cab we found. "It can get dangerous at night," Cody said. "Anything goes."

Cody told the cabbie to drop us off in front of an upstairs bar pumping out a distorted mixture of cheesy reggaeton and cheesier 1980s heavy metal. A man slumping in a chair was the lone occupant of the dance floor, and the waitresses, repeatedly pushing up their breasts with the palms of their hands, seemed to be on the happy hour menu. Cody said that most of the patrons were divers, but it was too loud to chat with any of them at the bar. The divers, however, did not find the volume an impediment. One got up and stood next to me. My apparent fame as an American in Bilwi had returned. "*Sandinistas, no me gustan* (I don't like Sandinistas)," he shouted, spitting into my ear. "I'd fight for America if they asked me to."

We walked along a moonlit road until Cody found a friend, Kuso, a lobster diver for seventeen years, at an open-air bar with uncharacteristically mellow music (perhaps a speaker wire had come loose). A free-diver (one who just holds his breath instead of using scuba gear), Kuso's naturally bronze skin radiated a youthfulness that ignored his forty-two years. We all split a tall bottle of Toña beer, over which he listed the prices for various qualities of lobsters, down to the illegal ones—small fry that haven't reached re-productive age—not worth very much but sellable if you find the right middleman. Since there is a regular ban last-ing four months of the year, there is pressure to make as much as you can during the other months. Kuso added that the divers instituted an additional ban on lobstering for the two months that followed Felix because "the water around the Cays was a cemetery."

In those two months, how did he survive? "Aid from America and Europe, mostly," he said. Did Nicaragua help? "Nicaragua cannot do much. Nicaragua is poor."

Why then does he dive, holding his breath for two minutes or longer, with ornery lobsters in tow? May fishing be an alternative? "Visiting the rock hotels makes the best money," he answered. The rock hotel is what the divers call a reef where lobsters live and hide. "I have to support my family. Clothing for the kids is expensive, especially for the girls."

THE DISPATCHER'S HANDIWORK had been tumbling around in a pot at Cody's place for three hours. We plucked the marinated shrimp off the barbecue, and we spooned up the turtle soup with its base of whatever coconut-pepper-fish stew had been left over from Cody's lunch. "It tastes like short ribs," I said of the odd-shaped joints, surprised by the rich meat's uncanny similarity. With full mouths, we nod-ded and laughed. It seems that if entrepreneurs wished to convert mud turtle into a luxury ingredient, they would only need to start exporting it and multiply its export price by ten. And maybe give it a French-sounding name.

LEST I WOULD THINK all bars in Bilwi are dives, Cody brought me to a discotheque writhing with young, perfumed, trilingual Miskito women studying at Bilwi's branch of the University of the Autonomous Regions of the Nicaraguan Caribbean Coast, and the collared-shirt boys who chase them. I didn't ask if at least some of the girls' fashionable clothes were paid for by scuba-diving daddies, but Flor de Caña, Nicaragua's top-shelf rum, was sure flowing faster than trade winds.

Cody introduced me to one of the few Westerners at the club, an American expat who had just hopped off the dance floor with his Miskito wife. He was tall and rosy-cheeked and stepped toward me. Then again, everyone looked rosy-cheeked in the glaze of the club's flattering light. "Welcome to paradise," he said to me in a blissful southern drawl. A thick hip-hop beat began jumping from the speakers. Before he could say more, and before I could say anything, his wife tugged him back to the dance floor.

FROM A WINDOW of the Managua-bound airplane, the zinc roofs of Bilwi, scattered around the coast, glistened in the sun like a spilled box of razor blades. It seemed to be a contradictory image—tools, capable of inflicting pain, covering a stunning landscape. When Rushdie wrote that "Beauty, in Nicaragua, often contained the beast," he was referring to the mountain forests that hid guerilla fighters during the Contra War. I thought of the plight of Bilwi's lobstermen on an idyllic coast; Rushie's reflection, written over two decades ago, had taken on new relevance.

The Seven-Córdoba Snapshot

The Leonese taught me the pleasures of riding a bus that takes you nowhere.

The Bus Pelon, the most popular route in Leon, Nicaragua, isn't supposed to take passengers anywhere, even though it passes through just about everywhere in the city before it brings everyone back to its starting point. It's Leon's very own version of cruisin', but with a diesel-spewing school bus replacing the muscle car.

Noting the lack of tourists in line for the Pelon, I grappled with the concept of why the folks of Leon would want to wait in a queue so they could pay seven córdobas and be shown their own city from the seat of a bus. The Pelon itself provided the first clue, for unlike regular Nicaraguan buses, the tires on the Bus Pelon, or "bald bus," are not the only bald parts: the back of the vehicle has no roof, owing to an encounter with a blowtorch.

The dog-breath air that groped me in the Parque Central provided the rest of the evidence. Such custom modifications to an old American school bus matched the needs of a low-lying, Central American city. In Leon, sweat owns the day. The Bus Pelon recaptures the night and creates a breeze where there is none.

A family of five in front of me. Nuns across the aisle. Handholding college students in flatteringly tight Colombian jeans everywhere else. Climbing the stairwell, kids waved at a sandwich cart beside the bus, and a drag queen in a taut t-shirt stopped slicing tomatoes and waved back.

The engine growled and we pushed through the air, forcing it to relinquish a little fresh comfort. The riders lacked a guide babbling facts through a mic—the Leonese wouldn't need that anyway—as the plaza revealed buildings so blackened with industrial belchfire that they appeared as photo negatives. The bald top was an advantageous viewpoint for checking out the city's blissfully decaying adobe-walled architecture, but the other riders cared little about sightseeing and busied themselves with the main activity on the Pelon, squirting water from plastic drinking bags on passersby. Such a selfless gesture, considering the climate. The bag squeezers scored a direct hit on a shaggy naked man stumbling in an aguardiente daze by the roadside as leaves of a low-lying branch whacked the staring nuns.

Beverages also provided the second-most popular activity: chucking empty soda cans off the bus. On the Pelon, there's no need to inconvenience your seatmate by reaching over him to stuff the can out the window, like on a regular Nica bus. You just fling it into the night. Socially aware littering.

Any self-respecting Central American city, no matter how small, boasts open plazas—a flaunting of a city's value on public space and community—and the Pelon managed to crisscross past most of its own. The community on the bus, a jiggling, giggling organism of rubbing hips, pumped the breeze full of college-age pheromones and non-stop quips in a chopped and greased-up Spanish sloppier than a twice-fried *fritanga*. My ordinary Spanish skills could not crack their code. Leon was the birthplace of the Sandinista revolution, and it was the first city liberated from the Somoza dictatorship; perhaps, at least in part, this was because the Somocistas could not understand intercepted transmissions from the Leonese rebels.

With the Pelon's social opportunities in full swirl, a few riders could not help themselves and signaled to the driver to stop because they wished to utilize the Pelon as a regular bus and get off along the route. Those party poopers just don't get it, do they?

For the rest of us, the Pelon compressed the city into an hour-long snapshot, blurred with an urban hum that refused to let hulking unemployment destroy its cheerfulness: church songs trickling from leprous adobe buildings; seismic reggaeton quarter notes testing the structural integrity of others; fireworks hand-fed into firing tubes in front yards (there's always some saint in need of a celebration in Nicaragua); a pair of lace panties discarded on a street corner, its adventures from the previous night tantalizingly untold.

Back at the central plaza, the line for the next Pelon ride disappeared deep into the square. The Museum of the Revolution, across from the sandwich maker's ever-quivering knife and luxurious eyelashes, attempted to sober up the line with "Bush = Genocide" graffiti scrawled across its façade. That afternoon, I had taken a museum tour with a guide who had himself been a Sandinista in the late 1970s during the revolution that overthrew dictator Anastasio Somoza. When he held up a replica of a homemade contact bomb—a taped-up ball of fertilizer and metal shards that was tossed by hand and exploded among the horrified faces of Somoza's troops—he announced, "We invented this." He indulged his nostalgia by showing me how he threw the bombs when he was a teenager.

And the Pelon? They invented that too. Rather than being designed to kill a dictator's minions, the Pelon kills perspiration.

I climbed down the Pelon's stairwell. But not everyone left the bus. The nuns stayed on, nodding in their hoods, yearning for another jaunt in the breezy cradle of Leon's mobile party. Or maybe they just wanted another look at the naked guy.

A Planet Within a Planet

Our first meeting began with an unexpected question: "Do you have socks?"

Tattooed and dressed in cargo shorts, Captain Karl Stanley stood before me in the sluggish morning heat of Roatán Island. He would be taking me to a depth of 2,000 feet underwater in his experimental vehicle, and the first question he asked me was if I had socks.

Thus began my earliest face-to-face conversation with the deep-sea submarine designer and captain. His inquiry added to a curious persona cultivated by several bar patrons I had met the night before on the island, Honduras' largest in the Caribbean, when I had mentioned that I was looking for him.

"His IQ is off the charts."

"To some, he may come off as aloof, but in reality he's just not that chatty."

"Karl's a little crazy, but in a good way. He just had a drink here. You just missed him."

The responses bloomed from behind bottles of Salva Vida beer as breezes from the Caribbean refreshed our brows. I worked my way down Karl's known haunts along the unpaved main road of West End, Roatán's scuba headquarters and home to the island's lively American expat community. Alas, I always seemed to be one beer behind him.

FOR SNORKEL AND SCUBA JUNKIES, Roatán has become synonymous with its beautifully bizarre reefs that lie just minutes from the coast. The island that once served as a place of exile—the British deported a community of Garifuna, a culture of mixed African and Amerindian descent, to Roatán in 1797—is now coveted for its natural treasures both above and below the surf.

The scuba-accessible reefs off the island's northern coast compose the uppermost reaches of a nearly vertical underwater trench, which lured Karl away from the States in 1998. He built his newest submersible specifically for the location's deep subterranean topography close to shore, offering us air-breathing creatures a window into depths where a wetsuit cannot go.

AFTER HAVING OBEDIENTLY DONNED a pair of sporty, below-the-calf socks, I waited for Karl at his submarine dock with photographer Lia Barrett for our scheduled dive. Lia, an American in her twenties, specializes in underwater photography and also lives on the island. Electricity had been

AWOL since morning, spurring a distant rattle of generators, a recurrent sound that I began to accept as part of the environmental din of the island.

The blue-green shallows of West End's Half Moon Bay crawled with groups of scuba instructors and their charges. I briefly reflected on how I could have been one of those students in a protected environment—a known method of undersea exploration. There's plenty of marvelous topography to investigate just a few meters down. But I had already been caught up in the spirit of the GO DEEPER block letters that Karl had painted on the roof over his submarine dock, as if to taunt the scuba students on the other side of the bay.

I swiveled to identify something airborne and closing in: a chiseled, bare-chested frame of a surfer, swooshing toward us on a zip line. That was our thirty-four-year-old captain, arriving from his house's second-floor balcony across from the dock. He was also the person with whom I had chosen to entrust my life in exchange for an opportunity to explore a little-known nether landscape and swap glances with lifeforms few humans, if any, had ever seen before. If his arrival represented the kind of adventurous-yet-unflappable nature Karl exploited to return safely from his over 1,000 previous sub dives, then he had my blessing.

We had already crawled into the snug confines of the three-person, 9,000-pound submersible, which he named *Idabel* after the town in Oklahoma where he welded it together, when I sensed a throbbing omission: the in-case-of-emergency briefing. Something like, "In case of evacuation, a compression suit can be found under your bench." Except that there is no such thing as a compression suit. I just made that up. The truth is that at 2,000 feet underwater, if something horrible happens, the best you can hope for is that you'll be instantly squashed like a grape in the name of science.

An almost-as-dubious scenario would be if the sub became stuck between large boulders. Who knows, a vessel from another part of the world might be sent to Roatán looking for the pinned sub (which is why he painted the sub bright yellow), but with so few vessels capable of the depths *Idabel* can achieve, salvation will most likely remain in the cheery territory of Hollywood scripts. Karl has furnished three days' worth of food and oxygen for the optimists.

I had initially thought the most logical rescue vessel would be Karl's first sub, a tubular, two-person submersible the inventor finished while in college (a rather practical extracurricular alternative to the chess club and spin-the-bottle), which he had taken on hundreds of dives without getting wet. But after a hurricane and complex negotiations sidelined both the sub's sale and donation prospects, Karl decided to decommission it. As we motored out of Roatán's Half Moon Bay, we passed over the first sub's final resting place, where Karl had intentionally sunk it. My imagined backup plan would have never sufficed, however, because unlike *Idabel*, his first submersible was not built to withstand the pressure at 2,000 feet.

From the acrylic viewing dome at the front, Lia and I looked straight up and watched the disk of wave-tossed daylight gradually shrink until blackness swallowed it. I felt the peculiar sensation of leaving the planet, even as we were probing deeper into it.

I believe the act of travel, at its most fundamental, is an exploration. But I have never felt the raw power of travel-fueled discovery more than when entering a place where one finds no light, no breathable oxygen, and no humanity. No tether connected us to the surface and the world we knew. And we were traveling to the ocean floor in a homemade submarine. Sure, we've all heard of homemade vehicles; soapbox racers come to mind. Maybe a pimped-out motorcycle. But a submarine?

I felt reassured when I tapped the half-inch thick, four-foot diameter steel sphere around Lia and me. I had expected it to ping metallically in response, but it didn't. Instead, I heard a dull pat. We could have been sitting in a hulky concrete alcove from the set of *A Clockwork Orange*.

A benefit to riding in *Idabel* (not that you can easily choose a mass-produced submersible instead) is that you ride with its creator, who had taken it on hundreds of dives. Karl, who had wanted to build submarines since he was nine, taught himself the technology and physics necessary for deep-water sub construction. He tracked down retired navy engineers who specialize in submarine research. The technology Karl had employed builds on the submarine's history spanning over three hundred years, albeit most of the submarine's evolution came about from military applications, including hand-steered suicide torpedoes and crude vehicles designed for drilling into hulls. Refreshingly, *Idabel* is armed with floodlights instead of warheads.

I turned around and met with Karl's bare feet. The sub's three spheres form an L shape, and Karl stood just behind us through the two vertically stacked spheres, where he operated toggle switches and controls in the topmost sphere. "Can you two lean forward a little? That would help us get down," Karl asked, demonstrating that even though the vessel weighs 9,000 pounds, it is so well balanced that the weight distribution of three people makes a difference.

With my tall frame and tiny camera sitting next to Lia's petite frame and large-barreled camera, it became obvious who was better suited to the confines of the forward sphere. But soon the emerging views would make me forget what my pain receptors, due to whatever kind of hunch-balled posture I had assumed, had been squawking about. At over 1,000 feet below sea level, the nothingness came alive as squadrons of tiny bioluminescent creatures burst into firework patterns inches in front of the dome. So omnipresent were the speck-sized organisms, dancing in a satiny ballet whose plot remains as puzzling as its characters, that they did not seem to be living in the water—they seemed to *be* the water. In their electrified theater, twitches of macaroni-sized shrimp and glowing wakes of jellyfish escorted our trip into their hauntingly peaceful playground, all to the soundtrack of soft engine murmur and a spacey Enya CD Karl was playing.

The sphere began to sweat with condensation from the colder water temperatures at the depths we were entering. Karl had asked that we take our shoes off before climbing in, and that we place our feet on bags of lead shot. The walls were clammy, but our feet were warm and dry. That's where the all-important socks came into play. I like a captain who looks out for the comfort of his passengers.

The depth gauge needle discreetly passed the 2,000 feet below sea level mark. Only half an inch of steel separated us from sixty times sea-level pressure, enough to crush a World War II-era German U-boat. But inside the sub, a chilly bubble, we still enjoyed the same pressure as when we were on the dock: one atmosphere. It felt like cheating

Mother Nature. In this stratum of permanent darkness, I hoped she wouldn't notice.

Karl followed the contours of the reef and gently positioned the sub in front of a boulder bustling with tight symbiosis: gangly crustaceans keeping guard around sponges, spiny pincushion creatures hiding under orange-red crinoids. The crinoids, whose sixteen limbs appear as sprigs of orange rosemary, are not plants, even though they appear as such (photosynthesis ceases a few hundred feet from the surface). While humans cannot survive in this realm, our hunger—both economic and gastronomic—has been known to send tools a lot less sophisticated than a submarine to such depths, thanks to trawling. The boulder was the kind of critter condo that could get wiped out with one unwitting pass of a trawler's jaws.

My hair dripped with condensation after grazing the top of the sphere. As Lia and I were feverishly examining and photographing the action on the boulder, the neighborhood was about to get more crowded. The floodlights captured an unmistakable outline approaching the sub. "Shark!" I yelled, which came out like an alarming bark, the only way to yell the word.

The six-gill shark, as long as the sub, took its time swimming toward us, vaguely entertained by our visit, offering a disturbingly expressionless stare. It circled us a few times before losing interest, but not before passing within a fin's length of the viewing dome and showing off a scar on its side that looked like bite marks from another shark.

If we had arranged for what Karl calls a "shark dive," the encounter might have ended up even cozier. For the shark dives, Karl purchases a pig head from the market at a nearby town and dangles it off a pole on the front of the sub. The passengers receive an unhindered view of the shark's dental health when it gorges on pig jowls just an arm's length from the sub.

The terrain began to border on fantasy. On flat patches of grey lunar sand, albino lobsters with two-foot antennae peeked out of their burrows. A lanky fish with the shine and shape of a sword floated perpendicular to the ocean floor, as if it were all that remained of a conquistador-era swashbuckler who thought he could slash his way past a shark. Karl had seen it before but still hasn't found its scientific nomenclature—that is, if any scientist has even classified and named it yet.

I asked Karl if he had shared his discoveries with the scientific community on the island. "We don't really have that here," he answered. I realized that the entire community I had asked about was standing behind me. Two thousand feet below and beyond: it's a region of ocean covering more than half the planet, yet it remains almost completely unexplored.

Karl found and approached something that not only has a name but whose genus' illustrated likeness already appears on t-shirts of the literary website McSweeneys.net: the Dumbo octopus. About the size of a grapefruit, this recently-discovered, shape-shifting comic relief of the deep resembled a purplish Gilligan hat someone dropped in the water, except for his big black eyes and ears that leisurely flap him across the sea bed. They're not actually ears; they're fins, but the Disney-esque nomenclature stuck. At one point he (she?) hunkered down on the sand in a flat blob—tucking in his stubby, pizza-dough legs—and moments later, he ended his vaudevillian skit by stretching into a bell shape to propel himself away, ear-fins flapping in sync.

A reverse aquarium: that's the only way I can describe it. Instead of the sea life being cooped up in a tank while landlubbers gawk and leave, we were the ones tightly sealed in while the creatures around us gawked at us and then disappeared into their immeasurable world. Of course, some of the creatures, having no need for eyesight in a dark void only lit by occasional bioluminescence, may have been blind and couldn't gawk at all, but probably smelled us with amused snorts from rubbery olfactory organs.

Somewhere between critters—maybe between the shark and the albino lobster—Karl had changed the musical selection to a Led Zeppelin mix, which matched our energy and awe levels. But soon we heard something more piercing than Jimmy Page's guitar solos: a hasty, violent hissing. It was too loud, too unnatural, too close to us to have originated from the sea floor. It came from the sub. I turned around to Karl and opened my mouth, but no words formed.

The noise stopped as quickly as it had arrived. "The sound you just heard was a high-pressure air leak," remarked Karl matter-of-factly, as when he'd said, "There's a cool jellyfish off the starboard side" just a few minutes earlier.

"How serious is that?" Lia asked in a rare glance away from her DSLR camera.

"Not a problem," Karl responded with a voice muffled from the closet-like acoustics of the sub. As he explained the operation of his ballast system in the same conversational tone—he inflates the ballasts with air to rise to the surface without the need of the motor-powered propellers—it was clear that the leak was minor and would not draw us to the three-day rations, nor would it even affect our speed to the surface. Robert Plant's scrotum-squished yelps didn't miss a note.

As Karl began a gradual rise to the surface, we rose up aside the wall of the trench, where terrain of sponge-covered boulders gave way to a rolling landscape of what Lia said resembled "snow-covered mountains." A Venus flytrap critter here, a bulgy-eyed langoustine cousin there. The longer we inspected a boulder, the more inhabitants appeared through the deliciously transparent waters, reframing my perspective of how humanity fits into this world.

The community wants the reef to remain as such. Due to lack of support from the Honduran government, local dive shops and businesses recently founded—and funded— the Sandy Bay West End Marine Park, an organization that now owns two boats and employs eleven staff members who protect the reefs from poachers and overfishing.

Curbing pollution remains another challenge. Roatán possesses just the kind of stunning, beach-studded coastline that makes absentee speculators salivate. More development will mean more waste. Underscoring the importance of the park's work, Karl's floodlights picked up a discarded toilet bowl resting sideways on a shelf about 500 feet below sea level. "That's the first time I've seen that," he said.

"The eastern part of the island is about to be ransacked by development," Lia mentioned. She was referring to the lands near the oldest communities of Garifuna, one of several cultures which make up Roatán's cultural fusion, along with recently arrived Hondurans from the mainland. Since the park's protection zone only wraps around the western-most point of the island, they are trying to expand their range.

In the meantime, Karl wants to keep sharing a literal window into a hidden part of our own earthly ecosystem, all while the inventor in him is continually experimenting, whether it's a new set of floodlights or a better way to hang the pig head off the sub. When he has trouble locating a new part for his ever-evolving submarine, he sometimes has friends coming to the island bring them in.

He even has a standing offer of half off his standard rate for anyone from *Idabel*'s county in Oklahoma to dive with him. He's had several takers already.

When the sub bobbed to the surface and the unapologetically bright Roatán sky splashed onto the dome, I was relieved that my eyes once again felt that tiny recoil of pain when adjusting to sudden sunlight. Two smiling boys from town waved to us from the dock, apparently not the first time they had enjoyed the uniquely Roatanian pastime of watching a submarine surface. Visions of ear-flapping octopi seemed like delusions or, at best, half-baked memories from a past life as an albino lobster.

Lia remarked that she had to go make a few "I'm alive" phone calls. I did too, but for me, they turned out to be more like "holy shit" calls, since what I'd just experienced had served as a humbling reminder of how much we don't know about our world and whom we share it with. I hadn't intended to hide the dangers that could plague a submarine, but while no dive is one hundred percent safe, what is? You could be smashed to an unsightly pulp by a drunk driver in the 'burbs when you return home after picking up a container of non-dairy creamer.

Thanks to Karl's experience, however, my largest concern of the day was a pair of socks.

Sissy Corn

It was five in the morning and already my feet were re-belling. The town's open-air stall for boots hadn't stocked anything large enough to fit me, and the used sneakers I had borrowed weren't much better, pinching my toes like oafish handshakes that wouldn't end.

Up before the roosters, marching through damp dark-ness, I was searching for the man who had lent me said foot-wear. But not to ask for a replacement. I was meeting him at a bus stop because I had volunteered to help him tend his corn crop for the day. I told myself the best way to learn about the life of the Ixil people of Nebaj, Guatemala, a town ravaged by the death squads of Guatemala's civil war that had ended twelve years ago, was to join the Ixil in their daily duties.

Through the black smear of unlit streets appeared a fig-ure carrying something on his back almost as large as him-self. It was hard to tell where the load ended and the human began. The word "unlucky" came to mind whenever I saw people from Nebaj slumping under bundles of firewood or vegetables or metal objects to be sold at the market.

I wondered what kind of load someone would be carrying at this hour. Ignoring my yelping feet, I ticked up my pace in an attempt to pass the man and scan the street for the farmer, Felipe. But in a quick, stooping waddle, the man blocked me. Breathing fast under a 100-pound bag of fertilizer, Felipe asked, "Are you ready?"

I'D FIGURED I COULD ASSIST Felipe because my parents had cultivated a corn crop, albeit a small one. The benefits of growing one's own food, however, had not seemed apparent to me at first. Like all the vegetables from our garden, our corn looked runty and homely next to the giant, uniformly colored produce from the supermarket. Our cobs grew a patchwork of white and yellow kernels, while the produce aisle's offerings obediently wore the same shade of bright yellow. Similarly, our carrots were stubby and gnarled and grew stringy beards. Our tomatoes abhorred roundness. The forces of American conformity were pressing hard on my pre-teen psyche. Were we doing something wrong?

Then I noticed how we always boiled the store-bought ears and drowned them in butter and salt, yet we ate the ears from our garden raw, each bite popping open the kernels' juicy, creamy sweetness. I tried eating a store-bought ear raw once, and almost gagged.

Sure, kids at school teased me when I told them I ate our garden corn raw. ("Ewww. You're weird!") But in choosing varieties of vegetables for flavor instead of shelf life and size, my parents were getting the kind of crop they had desired. Pass the runty vegetables, please. And don't boil 'em.

For my family, sweet corn meant more than dinner. When my father, brother, and I played Wiffle ball, the start of the corn patch served as the homerun line. We even named a lazy throw over home plate a "corn patch pitch." Always in view, the growing and wilting of the stalks ushered the seasons in and out. We always returned the cornhusks back to the garden in the compost pile. With the help of corn, we lived with the land in a small but palpable way, not just on top of it. I didn't realize the value of such a relationship until I went on to spend half my life living in urban environments where a layer of money has separated me from everything I've eaten. Except for a little thyme on the windowsill.

Just my luck—I was in a Guatemalan community where tortillas turn up during meals more often than utensils. Walk past open doors of Nebaj houses in the afternoon and you'll hear the pat-pat of fresh tortillas tossed between hands. Historically, corn held such importance for Nebaj's ancestors, the Maya, that they created their own corn god, Yum Kaax. The human-god-corn connection was deeper than that, however; according to one of the few remaining sacred Mayan texts, the *Popol Vuh*, the gods fashioned humankind from cornmeal (thankfully, they did not appear to use blue corn for this endeavor).

THE BUS, like many in Central America, was a hand-me-down from America's elementary school bus system. Its vinyl seats were full with ranchers and ranch hands traveling to their farms. The rims of their cowboy hats glowed with the orange embers of the sunrise, and the aisle was crowded with mud-caked boots poking from seats built for school-children. I felt like I was the only passenger on the bus who hadn't brought a bag of fertilizer.

We met Felipe's wife and two sons at the bus stop for his village, but we still needed another half hour to hike to his plot. My toes began curling in horror. Watching Felipe, though, I felt I had no reason to complain. Toting the 100-pound sack, Felipe never lost his shuffling rhythm, only stopping to bend down and swing his machete at a few branches along the path, hacking them off so they may be used as markers in his cornfield.

Soon the scenery of pigs, turkeys, cows, and flat cropland disappeared. We slid down a muddy path in the woods until a clearing ahead revealed a sharp drop-off. A few steps into the opening, I gazed out at the goose-bump view of the other side of the valley, revealing crops clinging to the slopes between tufts of trees. Felipe didn't seem too interested in the view and busied himself unstrapping the fertilizer sack. This was because we were standing in Fe-lipe's corn crop, on the side of a mountain steeper than a stiletto pump. The land wasn't terraced; he had planted the stalks right into the mountainside. It seemed that footwear was no longer my most pressing concern, excepting a sudden desire for crampons.

Felipe chopped a point on the end of a stick. He showed me how to dig a little hole in the dirt near the stalk with the point of the stick and put in fertilizer using a plastic cooking oil jug cap as a measuring cup. When he dug, I noticed he was turning over black soil. His motions released a dense, sweet puff of earthy air around us. The soil looked healthy. Why bother with the expense of fertilizer?

"I'll use it only for a few years more," he answered. "The land is still mud." When I wobbled down the rows he assigned to me, I found isolated patches of the mud to which he had been referring. Or I should say my feet had an uncanny talent for finding them all, each time sending me a few rows down until I managed to hit an exposed tree stump. The real trick to sliding, once I ignored pesky messages from my survival instinct, was to do it while keeping the bowl of expensive fertilizer from spilling, without dropping the cap (lest it roll down the mountain disturbingly faster than a fleeing iguana), and without flattening stalks on the way down. I learned to use the digging point more as a walking stick in an effort to keep me in the same row.

On the hike, we had passed field after field of flat corn crops, fields that could probably be harvested while driving a tractor. Or while wearing flip-flops. I tried not to let myself be distracted by envious thoughts of the farmers who worked flat land, who tended their easy corn. Their sissy corn.

Meanwhile, Felipe was crouching through his rows without wobbles or slides. His wife Catarina, with infant son strapped to her back, fertilized the steepest part of the patch, about forty-five degrees, which bordered a gouge-like drop-off that led straight to a distant stream below. The infant must have served as a kind of magic ballast.

I remained in a perpetual war with balance. I kept swaying like a drunkard, my feet failing to find anything flat to stand on. Because of such absence of equilibrium, my head felt as if it weighed as much as a sack of fertilizer. Meanwhile, I observed Felipe's older son, six-year-old Tito, who kept filling up our bowls and almost never slipped. His lower center of gravity inspired me to crouch down and walk around the mountain with my knees tucked into my chest. It became clear that being tall is not a beneficial trait for working a mountain crop.

Crouching brought me much closer to the soil that squirmed with life. When I scratched open holes in the surface, bugs with various leg counts became annoyed that I was tearing the roofs off their highways and scurried back into the dampness. In addition to his plot being bordered on two sides with forest, Felipe left a few scrawny trees standing in the middle of his plot, sacrificing a minimum amount of sun while providing a stream of falling, decaying leaves that fed the busy cast of critters in the earth below. The soil smelled dark, moist, and rich. Every time I slipped and fell, I smelled dark, moist, and rich. It was a reassuringly familiar smell, though. As if the land said to me, "Welcome back."

By now, the sneakers were piranhas locked on my feet, biting but not quite able to swallow their catch. For some reason, though, I didn't care about the pain anymore. I had fallen into a tight rhythm of crouching, digging, and pouring. From across the valley, tinny wafts of amplified guitar drifted toward us, steadying our pace with the same dreamy melody played over and over again. Felipe said it was coming from a Mayan church, but I was left to wonder what kind of religion would be playing the same chorus for hours, since the trance-like music seemed more appropriate for keeping ranch hands working.

I once again doubted his need for fertilizer, but then again, I am not the one who needs to live off of the corn from this plot. His plot is not a commercial venture—it will supply his family with tortillas for all of next year.

And speaking of tortillas, we had just finished our work, and Felipe gathered us all at the top of the plot so we could eat—not surprisingly—tortillas. As the crop would not be ready for harvest for another five months, the tortillas he brought were made from the cornmeal from his crop from the previous year. We dipped them in a tomato salsa and washed them down with coffee.

As I perched myself on the slope, legs straddling a fledgling corn stalk, I felt energized, maybe even intoxicated, by plugging into the pulse of rural Guatemala's food cycle. The farther we move away from that pulse, the easier it is to forget that we, the clever creatures we are, can inadvertently dismantle the life-giving cycle with pesticides and profits. Sure, we might circumvent the need for the food cycle and someday discover a way to digest things like rocks and discarded Ziploc bags (now *that* would be clever), but I'll still cast my vote for corn because it tastes better.

The guitar kept up its smooth resolve, the cows down in the valley below looked like lazy mites, and I began to understand why Felipe, who lives near the bustle of Nebaj, chose to grow his crop here, an hour from his home, on a slope where one's shoes will never find even footing. "It's more tranquil here," he said while mopping up the salsa with the edge of his tortilla. From decaying leaves to tortillas, Felipe found his own connection with the land. And he accomplished it without a Wiffle ball diamond.

While I tucked away tortilla after tortilla, one pestering thought threatened to ruin the moment: mountain corn tastes just like sissy corn. Of course, there is no logical reason for a difference as long as the seeds, the soil, and the tending methods are similar. But after a morning of mountainside vertigo, I had hoped his tortillas would set off otherworldly fireworks in my mouth. The temperament of Yum Kaax seems to follow science more than whim. What kind of god is that?

I did manage to find a difference, albeit not a gastronomic one. The piranha shoes had been somehow defanged, their gummy nibbling barely noticeable under the soreness humming through a variety of stretches of my body. All the slips and ankle twists must have helped to break in the shoes. I seemed to have discovered a hidden benefit of mountain corn.

Back in Nebaj that afternoon, I bought an ear of grilled corn, garnished with a lime wedge, from a street vendor who was working over a portable charcoal pit. Using nothing more than pocket change to acquire the corn cob, I felt like the ultimate sissy.

The Sound of Good Fat

The tropical sun could no longer reach me. I had fallen into nut therapy.

I was not following a nouveau spa trend, although I would not be surprised if owners of such establishments take note. I was sitting in the shade of a macadamia orchard in the Guatemalan highlands, listening to ripe nuts falling onto the ground. Each time a breeze rolled down the cones of the encircling volcanoes and teased the treetops, I absorbed the vibrations of a warm thump from somewhere—another nut's fall broken by soft, dark soil. Nature's tom-toms, soloing over a woodlands jam session. Improvisation for wind and branch.

Some people flock to the beaches to listen to the swish of the surf to relax. Others may seek the sweet jibber-jabber of birds. I stumbled upon a like-minded yet less-celebrated source just a short bus ride from the buzz of Antigua, Guatemala's most visited city. I had been ready to interview

Lawrence Gottschamer, the founder of the organic macadamia orchard known as the Valhalla Experimental Station—a farm that gives macadamia seedlings to the indigenous people of Guatemala as an alternative to unsustainable farming practices—when the magnetic patter of ripeness struck.

"You have to make a mess of this," remarked Lawrence, his silver beard quivering, his fingers twirling in a playful swat. The words snapped me back to the table and drew my focus toward a plate of pancakes in front of me. A neat zigzagging of macadamia nut butter topped the pancakes and begged for the uncouth kind of christening that Lawrence recommended.

Lawrence was never one for pandering to conventionalism anyway. The existence of a thriving crop of macadamia trees in the middle of Guatemala—halfway around the planet from the tree's origins in Australia—demonstrates the success of his creative methods. Over thirty years ago, he was recruited to assist in finding a way to grow macadamia trees in Costa Rica. He had served in Vietnam and had been retired in the line of duty as a fireman when he was tapped. "The word 'no' is not big in the fireman's vocabulary," he explained. "The requirements were that I had no experience with macadamias and no Spanish."

He made his first discovery shortly after he was told that growing macadamia trees at sea level in the tropics was impossible. He walked into the jungle to relieve himself and came close to watering a soaring macadamia tree growing in the wild. No one knows how the tree got there. The nuts float, so it's possible one had washed up from across the Pacific.

Narrating between mouthfuls of his own blissfully sloppy pancakes, he recounted moving to Guatemala in 1976, where he took note of the devastation caused by slash-and-burn farming—desiccated landscapes that can no longer support crops. He then inherited forty years' worth of macadamia research from California botanists, and started breeding trees that have been naturally adapting to Guatemala's mountainous, volcanic soil. He has been cultivating his own varied stock of seeds since.

Conventional wisdom also claimed that farmers needed to graft their macadamia trees. Grafting requires cutting shoots from a master tree and grafting them onto a rootstock of a different variety, resulting in all trees being genetically identical, since the rootstock's genes don't reach up to the fruit. Yet we sat among 300 macadamia trees, all of which were grown from the farm's own seeds without grafting. "Every tree is different," Lawrence remarked.

He explained why we should care whether the trees are clones or not. Clones produce uniformly sized nuts, easier for a machine to harvest, and they are bred to have high yields. The problem comes when the blight comes. A crop containing a single variety of a plant—a practice called monoculture—can be wiped out by a single blight. Just ask the Irish, whose use of monoculture contributed to their nineteenth-century potato famine.

The United Nations Food and Agriculture Organization estimates that seventy-five percent of our food crop's genetic diversity has been eliminated in the past century. "It's genetic suicide," Lawrence spat. I tend to believe that innately; we understand the importance of genetic diversity because if we didn't, we'd all be marrying our siblings. Anyone up for more royal hemophiliacs?

To make up for a monoculture crop's inability to defend itself, farmers hose it down with pesticides and fungicides, effectively killing the soil and requiring the addition of chemical-based fertilizer. Some insects nonetheless "resist the spraying and survive, and then become congress people," Lawrence commented. Diverse crops not only survive in soil rich in microbes and fungi, they can thrive in it—without the need for chemical fertilizer that can end up polluting rivers with their runoff. Such moist, clumpy, living, bustling soil also becomes its own defense against wind erosion. And it provides an uncannily tuned drumhead in the company of falling nuts.

Since Valhalla has been giving away free seedlings to Guatemalan farmers, I wondered how many of those farmers were also enjoying pancakes with macadamia butter from their own harvests. "In one village, for example," explained Lawrence, "I gave away seedlings to twenty-five families. Twenty-four were failures. One family has a thriving orchard and sells nuts to the others." I had already noticed that baskets of the nuts have been turning up in markets around the country alongside the usual Guatemalan fare of chicken feet and tamales, although macadamia pancakes still have a long way to go to dethrone *gallo en chicha* (rooster in a thick sauce made from fruit wine) as the special of the day.

"Have you gotten the tour yet?" Lawrence asked, waving me to join him for a walk toward an open-sided structure that buzzed with the nasally whirl of a motor. "You're gonna like this." A cloud of debris circled the building. One of the farmers was pouring ripe macadamias, still with their green husks, into a rebar track around a wheel taken from a truck. The tire, bald and spinning in a furious blur—long since retired from navigating landslides along Guatemalan highways—gripped the nuts, violently ripped off their husks against the track, and shot the recognizable hard shells, brown and round, onto a collecting table. What was that sweet gas smell? Aha—a lawnmower engine powered the wheel.

Tracing the path of the nuts through the dehusker, I felt the same consuming fascination as when I used to follow the metal ball through the mismatched pieces of the *Mouse Trap* board game as a child. And that's when I began to appreciate the simplicity of the device. The ranch built the dehusker out of scraps commonly found around any farm in Guatemala. That was the intent—to show farmers that they can build one too.

"Look at all the sizes," he shouted over the clanking, his eyes wide and hovering. He brushed his fingers through the table's nuts, ranging in diameter from cherries to ping-pong balls.

With hundreds of shells rolling around before me, I considered the many impacts of the farm. Besides my newly found percussive source of solace, the nuts carry the advantage of providing a farmer with a year-round food source, giving welcome stability in a country that had emerged from a devastating civil war in 1996. When a farmer only grows coffee (a common practice in Central America), the beans can't be eaten if their price drops. Macadamias, more than just an indulgent snack with a velvety crunch, provide protein and omegas. Most of the fats are monounsaturated in a higher proportion than even olive oil.

I stepped over a layer of scattered husks while sweet echoes of the macadamia butter's richness still rippled on my tongue, still pampered my consciousness. I reflected on how such a treat could be so beneficial. With tragic frequency, foods that agree with one's health or the health of the environment may not be so agreeable to the palate. The gullets of the health-conscious often have to reckon with flavor-free rice cakes, or dumpster-scented noni juice, or multigrain muffins suspiciously reminiscent of old wood chips.

While the nut harvests provide food and income for farmers across Guatemala (augmented by Valhalla's aim to buy as many nuts from the farmers as it can), it's the nut's oil that has attracted international attention. Lancôme, a Paris-based cosmetics company, uses an extract from Valhalla's nuts as the active ingredient in their anti-aging treatment. "The process of extraction is so secret, it's not even patented," Lawrence gloated. That's because he possesses a more effective safeguarding of his intellectual property than what a piece of paper can provide: he made sure to mention to me that Valhalla's machete-brandishing farmer who performs the extraction process is equally skilled in relieving trespassers of their scrotums.

Picking up the anti-aging oil at the gift counter, I wondered how many castrated spies went into the making of each bottle. Less mysterious but just as important in showcasing the crop's versatility were chocolate-covered macadamias, bars of macadamia oil soap, and bottles of the aforementioned macadamia nut butter, all packaged with the mantra *"Hagamos del Planeta Tierra nuestra iglesia y protegerlo nuestra religion"* (Let's make planet earth our church, and protecting it will be our religion).

While his son Ricardo explained the benefits of sustainable agriculture to a group of tourists, Lawrence pulled me aside and said, "I shouldn't be in business. This project is a response to problems. The idea is to transfer the technology to the local people." They were humble words coming from the world's leading expert in sustainable macadamia farming. They were words that sounded as enchanting as the song of an edible orchestra. Lawrence seemed to know this already, because he pointed out several molded basins dug into a hillside that looks out onto Guatemala's wavy spine; the construction work is part of an outdoor hot tub he is building in the middle of his orchard, where the ambient beats are always dialed in.

Fight, Flight, or Boogie

The figure before me looked runty in his oversized throne. But with one expectant hand out, palm up, he made his intentions clear. I was standing in someone's living room in the highlands of Guatemala, wondering how long I'd have to wait for my request to take effect. I was new to this petitioning-a-saint thing.

Perhaps I wasn't petitioning San Simón so much as bribing him. I had taken a cue from about a dozen followers, seated in rows in front of him, who'd poured flasks of sugarcane hooch down his wooden throat. His 80-proof pee would be collected in a bowl and sold to believers as holy, if not slightly kinky, tonic. As one might guess, San Simón, also known by his Mayan name, Maximon, is not your standard-issue saint who peers out from a humble face and whose statue remains roped off from the rabble of humanity, separating the consecrated from the sinning.

His face hidden behind a bandanna, his head topped with a cowboy hat, the rest of his body poking through a pin-striped gangster suit, San Simón is the patron saint of vice. In a country boasting an assortment of specialized Mayan gods in charge of everything from corn to fertility, the generic powers of the Christian god, the newcomer on the block, must have seemed bland in comparison. And offered little for gamblers. Somewhere in the unintended wrinkles of conquest, as legend has it, the spirit of a priest known for living with and standing by the indigenous people of Guatemala cross-pollinated with the power of Mayan divinity. The result was a saint who exists among the people and has the same tastes for life's pleasures. Defender of the common man.

Several towns in Guatemala's highlands dress up their respective San Simóns in badass threads. Here, in Zunil, the dapper mannequin is mobile. Like a traveling carnival, the life-sized, hand-carved likeness, whose shrine comes complete with an arch of fluorescent bulbs and garlands, is carried to a new home every year. Families wait for years for the honor of looking after him. Unsurprisingly, with his hand out and a sneer hardening his upper lip, San Simón has never found himself inside Zunil's church. I visited the church earlier that afternoon and met with the usual solemn pews, the building's most festive focal point being a sculpture of Jesus riding a pony, tempered by another featuring him haloed and bleeding, his puppy-dog eyes asking, "Why me?"

San Simón, with his gruesomely festive shrine, doesn't seem to be caught up in such philosophical quandaries. When I had first arrived at the house, curious to see why the town keeps returning to his aura, I found a woman in

snug jeans kissing his cheek and nuzzling his painted ear-
lobe, which led to her candy-coating a whisper. Another lip-
sticked petitioner stroked his jaw while begging for something in the indigenous K'iche' language, hitting a low,
sultry register I hadn't heard before in the tongue. He's
been dead for centuries, and he's still a chick magnet. Sure,
the petitioners could simply promise to be good people in
exchange for a wish. But what does the saint get out of it?
"Nothing's free," San Simón's posture declares.

While he can't vocalize anything, his handlers care for
him as if he were an invalid uncle. They change his clothes.
They position his arms on the armrests. They decorate the
table in front of him with bottles of liquor and a creepy arrangement of mini-Simón figurines.

But with his sunglasses and bandanna hiding the glare
on his varnished face, he almost appeared lifelike. As if he
could get up out of his chair and sort out the faithful from
the fakers with a barroom fist.

That was not why I had decided to make an offering.
When I had begun to suspect that the others were wondering why I was standing there watching the saint and his en-
tourage, I figured I should try to blend in and make a wish
as well. Wishing is what people came for, after all. They did
not come to be observed by a curious foreigner (although,
as a foreigner, I had to pay admission as an introductory
offering).

Like the others before me, I purchased a flask of 80-proof
aguardiente from the adjoining store, its proximate convenience no accident. When I returned to the shrine, a woman
in a long, geometrically patterned dress and leather loafers
was already waiting for me behind San Simón. She pulled
down his bandanna and tilted his chair backward, her fluid

command of the metal throne's mechanics speaking of a well-practiced routine. A member of the family caring for San Simón for the year, she was ready to midwife yet another divine transaction, albeit with the slight wandering glance of a grocery store cashier on autopilot.

Somewhere behind the throne, a radio played a cheerful melody blending marimba and what resembled polka— one of Guatemala's home-grown musical styles that draws from Afro-Guatemalan influences and colonial-style marching bands. It was music that said, "That's right, we're not in church, live it up."

The fluorescent bulbs mocked reality with their unnatural brightness, chilling the concrete walls. Fitting, actually. With a bottle in my hand and San Simón's eager lips before me, the absurdity of what I was about to do made me hesitate and tighten my grip. I could not hide from what can often be the selfish side of praying for divine intervention. Let me illustrate the point with the following scenario. Imagine a farmer praying for rain to save his parched crop, while an engaged couple, to be married in a park next to the farm, fold their hands together for a sunny day. If the deity indulges one of them, the recipient of good tidings knowingly ends up harming the other. In other words, screw thy neighbor.

Flexing one's self-interest, however, seems appropriate and even encouraged when standing before a wooden-livered saint whose handlers charge an admission fee. Years of Catholic high school had tried to instill in me the idea that Christians should be humble. I've noticed that such a notion, in practice, often ends up evaporating into a thin, polite veneer around one's true desires, which is one of the reasons why I lost touch with organized religion. But in the house of San Simón, prayer had stripped itself down to honest, me-first essentials.

Then came the hard part. What to wish for? Whom did I wish to screw over? I tried to envision an outcome that would not disadvantage too many people. Coming from the United States, I reflected on my awkward position. Even my wobbly dining room table in my Queens apartment was more than many folks seemed to have in Zunil. I could not muster up the requisite gluttony, and I felt bad asking for anything at all. Nor did I feel particularly evil at the moment.

I decided to donate my wish to the cause of the Guatemalan people. I wished that every Guatemalan, regardless of class, family tree, or penchant for cockfights, could have a drink if they so desired, whether they could afford it or not. I figured booze was something San Simón could provide.

When my wrist emptied the last of the flask, I noticed a woman, hair well-coiffed, holding a lit cigarette behind me. The handler had barely tilted San Simón back up in his chair when the woman stuffed the cigarette into his mouth. A polka supercharged with a manic merengue rhythm bounded off the cinderblocks, yet San Simón, in perfect form, refused to ruin his commanding posture with even a toe tap. I wondered if the cigarettes would be resold as tools of holy appetite control.

I walked to the back of the room and sat next to Ramón, a construction company owner who leaned forward in his chair and could not stop grinning. He nodded as if both of us were members of a secret society, members who were fiendishly clever enough to have discovered the same source of power. I asked Ramón why he visited. "He brings good luck," he said. "He's good for business."

Curious as to how the saint has treated the rest of Zunil, I left the shrine and walked along the cobblestone streets between the town's skinny, trapezoidal houses. I found a disproportionate number of storefronts for a small town, painted in inescapably bright colors that brought dead concrete to life. An arcade with battered video game machines, a dentist advertising gold teeth coverings more for aesthetics than prosthetics, a typing school spilling metallic percussion from an open-air classroom—I am sure Ramón would have assured me that their success was due to repeated petitions with firewater.

The afternoon sun was already creeping down toward the mountains. The streets smelled of grilled tortillas and sweet smoke from burning firewood, and kitchens clanked with pots and swirling spoons. I still wanted to explore more of the town, but I knew the buses back to the city of Xela (also known as Quetzaltenango), where I was staying, would stop running soon, so I stepped into the nearest storefront, a bar on the road to the bus stop, to ask when the last bus would be departing.

The bartender presided over a domain the size of a garage, with matching ambience. His only three customers were huddled in a corner. Just before I reached the bar, I felt a bony hand tugging at my wrist. Knotty extremities emerged from her layers of mismatched fabric. Her eyes were sunk into her face but still probed with steady purpose. She stomped in a deliberately halting, sloppy rhythm, indicating that I had just stepped onto a dance floor, and I was expected to partake.

As I edged toward the bar, I matched her steps, slop for slop, and even threw in some disco-esque sways. The woman gasped and giggled, apparently never having seen such moves. I hadn't, either, since I was making the whole thing up. The bartender seized on the action and turned up his tape player, sending another of Guatemala's bouncy marimba polkas about the concrete walls.

She pointed to a man standing behind her. "That's my papa!" she screeched. He offered me his raspy grip. The father-daughter duo smiled in chorus and displayed the roughly eleven teeth they shared between them. I would never again have a chance to refine my count, for the father sealed shut his change-purse lips and began inspecting me as if I were on an audition. But for what?

The only other bar-goer was her younger sister, whose wraps of fabric revealed a baby strapped to her back. Her pudgy cargo did not stop her from sucking on a cigarette with one hand and pushing her sibling further into me with the other. San Simón's kind of people.

I ran out of dance moves, and I began feeling time drip off me like sweat, so I darted toward the bar, ordered a beer, and asked the bartender if he knew the bus schedule. I figured the older sister, introduced to me as Nilda, would stop dancing if she saw me taking a beer break. But she kept clawing at my arm, yelping, *"Estados Unidos!"* (United States).

The bartender, keen to share a moment with a refreshingly sober customer, shrugged with an apologetic half-smile and told me I had twenty minutes until the last bus left. The gentleman I am, I offered to buy my dance partner a drink as well. Or at least that was how I had hoped my gesture would appear. It was another of my attempts to keep her from dancing and pawing at me. The bartender fetched the same brand of aguardiente with which I had indulged the local saint.

Like several other Guatemalans I had met, the bartender mentioned to me that a few of his children were working in the United States. I began to respond that his children's enthusiasm for Americans was presumably not quite as intense as Nilda's, but the only syllable that came out was "Ow!" because Nilda had grabbed my pinky and bent it in ways it wasn't intended to go. "Look! My papa!" she shouted through squeaky laughter.

And what did her papa think of such behavior? He pointed a finger at me, his knuckles swollen and bulby. "Dance," he commanded. His single word shot out in a booming blurt, as if he had told me to sit, stay, or roll over.

I managed to wrestle my pinky free and tried to muster up a few more moves. While stepping toward the door, I disguised my departure in a flurry of pseudo salsa, some out-of-place ska arm pumps, and a series of hideous robot maneuvers (her favorite). The family ate it up. And so did the crowd that had grown around the bar's entrance. Since the bar lies on the road to the bus stop, Zunil's main artery, the commuters had been passing by the open door, gazing in with insatiable rubbernecker eyes.

They watched a performance that would have repelled mojito-sipping ladies in any East Village dance club by the dozens. But, well, I wasn't in New York anymore. No matter how bad I thought I looked, I had them hopelessly engrossed, such a surprising ego boost delivered by the mad chemistry of cultural face-offs that travel can unexpectedly provide. On a cold, dusty concrete floor in the mountains of Guatemala, robot moves rule.

But surely they will soon grow tired of me? *"Estados Unidos!"* she squealed again, causing me to remember the observation—one that I had deemed insignificant—that in addition to his pinstripes and bandanna, San Simón had worn an American flag across his shoulders when I had seen him.

"Dance!" Papa commanded.

In back of the bobbing head of the younger sister, the baby's drool dripped from his lips. I reflected on Nilda's lack of children in tow, perhaps due to a lack of a suitor, and that her father seemed to have found a solution to that problem with my arrival. Aren't we moving things too fast?

Her younger sister didn't think so, shoving her sibling into me again. "Take a picture of you two," she yelled. When I declined, an odd sensation seized me, a feeling the indigenous folks from the highlands of Guatemala might reckon with when a tourist wants to take their picture. With my exotic cargo pants and size 10½ double-wide sneakers, I was something to stare at. Something to photograph. I was beginning to see myself the way the locals saw me. As if it were a message from the *defender of the common man*.

A neat trick from a saint with a snappy wardrobe, I thought. As the family unceremoniously shared and guzzled the contents of the bottle I had bought for Nilda, I considered the thought that in buying the bottle, the wish I had made in front of San Simón seemed to have been granted, at least for these folks. Counting myself as a scientifically minded person not partial to hocus pocus—no matter how romantic the thought of a paranormal hand tweaking what the human hand cannot, adding fairness and hope when reality cares not—I dismissed such possibilities. Besides, no one was getting screwed over, right?

Nilda grabbed both of my pinkies and twisted them, pulling them like reigns. *"Estados Unidos!"*

"Dance!"

The more I struggled to free myself, the more she enjoyed it. Giggle by giggle, the fight shook loose the little girl from inside her, blossoming from under a sunbaked face. In her grin that puckered her eyes, softening her sharp Mayan cheekbones, I began seeing her years wind backwards, with all the jugs of food carried on her head taken off, all the harvested corn placed back in the stalks, all the lollypop-destroyed teeth growing back.

Meanwhile, the pain in my hands reminded me of my current predicament. The last bus would be leaving soon.

What a team player, that bartender. He switched off the tape mid-marimba solo, smacking the walls with jarring silence. Nilda jerked up her head. Her stare, a reflex of a stare starting with irritation and morphing into guilt, thrashed from me to the bartender and back to me. Nilda, the grown-up Nilda, released my hands. The child Nilda vanished deep into faded layers of fabric.

I hesitated for a moment, the length of which I cannot recall, for the sake of the child Nilda, perhaps also for the kid in me. The kid who lives for hideous robot dancing.

"There's no more music. Sorry, can't dance anymore!" I said with a theatric shrug. I caught the bartender's eyes for a nodding thank you, and I walked out to the road.

When I climbed aboard the bus to Xela, the noisy din of Spanish and K'iche' collapsed into whispers. Eyes turned to me. I realized that the people on the bus had seen me in the bar on their walk to the bus stop. I found a seat and tried to hide, but a woman in front of me turned around and asked, "Did you enjoy your dance?"

Some might say, blissfully and self-assuredly, that I met with the power of prayer. Others will spout, didactically and patronizingly, that buying gifts for a painted manne- quin is a waste of time. Such is wrestling inside the inher- ently inconclusive caverns of faith.

I turned to the window. The sun had just ducked behind the mountains as the bus began its climb toward Xela. The scent of grilled tortillas somehow blew in from town and entered the bus, an unlikely feat, but not impossible.

Intermission #2: Barbecue-flavored Mealworms

Have you ever been to a zoo where you are encouraged to peek into the monkey cages and then, at lunchtime, the cafeteria serves you flame-grilled monkeyburgers? That's the kind of perversely confident "we're at the top of the food chain" outlook that the Montreal Insectarium exercises once a year at their annual insect tasting. I figured that, since I've kissed lipstick made of crushed-up cochineal bugs (like it or not, most lipsticks are made from them), over the years I've been priming myself for a dish of honey-roasted crickets or caterpillar ceviche. But how do I pull off a wine pairing without looking like an unrefined slob?

Fortunately, the insectarium spared me such dinner-table anxiety because they had canceled this year's tasting. I had to settle for a box of dried, barbecue-flavored mealworms from the gift shop. Such a setback was like expecting roast suckling pig and ending up with a bag of fried pork rinds, although the literature inside the box promised that its contents occupied a loftier place on the gastronomic totem pole. "Mealworms are the stars of our insect tastings and can be prepared in lots of different ways. They are generally used to replace nuts, raisins or chocolate chips in many recipes."

Before I threw them into cookie batter, I felt I should sample a few straight from the box. They were weightless and resembled Cheetos that forgot to puff up. So wispy were the mealworms that I needed three or four in my mouth at a time to actually feel like I was chewing on something, and that's when I met with a fiery saltiness followed by a surprisingly luxurious finish of tobacco. Perhaps an up-and-coming competitor to Nicorette?

Showdown at the West Esplanade Canal (a.k.a. Breakfast for Alligators)

xciting events are not supposed to happen in the suburbs. I mean, what would the neighbors think?

So I wondered what the neighbors thought as I cruised past their curtained living rooms while shell casings flew in front of my nose. It was midnight, and I was sitting in the back of a pickup truck between a two-man SWAT team that was blasting away at an insidious foreign invasion threatening to destroy New Orleans.

The invaders, from the lawless jungles of South America, are not aware of their transgressions. That's because they are large, furry rodents called nutria. What's worse, they did not choose to invade America; Americans had brought them here. Imported in the 1930s for their luxuriously soft coats, they were released from farms in southern Louisiana when the price of the fur was low. Now that wearing rodent has fallen out of vogue, the fur is almost worthless. Millions of litters later, the creatures have been ravaging the wetlands that protect New Orleans from storm surges, munching up vegetation with their unsettlingly orange buckteeth and leaving nothing but mud behind. The state now pays five dollars for each tail to encourage eradication—but not a penny for the fur—and has attracted few hunters.

More recently, some nutria, perhaps preferring a nicer neighborhood for raising their young, have moved into the 'burbs around New Orleans. But instead of taking advantage of the well-funded school systems, the rodents, averaging twelve pounds apiece, have been chewing up and burrowing into banks of the city's canals, destabilizing levee walls, and disrupting drainage in a city that lies mostly under the level of the ever-eager Lake Pontchartrain. Hurricane Katrina made the lake's intentions clear.

If the nutria were left to do what they do best, America would not need another hurricane to undermine the levees. The Jefferson Parish Sheriff's Office, however, is not about to let that happen. The truck I was jostling around in had prowled the same route many times before, including along the infamous Seventeenth Street Canal, where a breach during Katrina in 2005 had flooded most of downtown New Orleans. "We've been shootin' these canals since 1995," Major Kerry Najolia, overseer of the nutria eradication effort, mentioned to me, not without pride, when he drove me to meet the SWAT team.

His Crown Vic now followed the pickup, along with another truck, the carcass cleanup crew, forming the three-vehicle caravan of death. My shoes slipping on shell casings, I asked the baggy, camo-outfitted team what it's like being paid to hunt. "We're just tryin' to help out before something bad happens," Officer Sparky answered, a clump of tobacco bulging inside his lip. "They quick fellas, too." He spit into his makeshift spit cup, an empty bottle of Coke, while aiming a spotlight at the other side of the canal along West Esplanade Avenue, part of Jefferson Parish's 300 miles of drainage waterways. Sleeping strip malls and single-family homes trustingly overlooked both sides, while Officer Mark aimed his scoped Ruger .22 on the spotlight, searching for telltale damage above the waterline indicating what they call "nutria condominiums."

We crept past a peaceful midnight scene of Americana—cul-de-sacs and backyard barbecue grills in the glaze of a light-bulb moon. These were the kind of houses harboring baseball card collections and potpourri bowls and toasters that create images of the Virgin Mary. It didn't seem like a natural setting for squeezing off rounds.

Then the spotlight found the condominiums, networks of holes gouged into the canal bank, complete with a few pudgy balls of brownness lounging around as if moonlight nourished them. Nutria, *Myocastor coypus*, champions of chowing down, losers of beauty contests.

Above them, brickfaced houses nuzzled up to the canal. We were so close that I could see the curly metal trim around the doorbell buttons. Mark signaled for the driver to stop. "Yup, that's a condominium," Sparky remarked with unruffled inflection, as if he had said, "Yup, the train's on time." The .22 reported a deceptively short pop.

I kept reflecting that it's not the nutria's fault. They are just doing what nature intended, although nature never intended for them to do it on this continent. Inhaling gunpowder smoke and watching the cleanup crew collect the vanquished with a garden rake (the action spotlighted like a circus act gone wrong), I could not help but ponder how the answer to the nutria invasion has come down to this.

There used to be another answer: our stomachs. In 1998, in the wake of the fur market collapse, the state of Louisiana promoted the eating of nutria meat, which has more protein and less fat than beef. Since nutria only eat vegetables and roots, their meat is clean and healthy, meat that chef Paul Prudhomme of K-Paul's Louisiana Kitchen began serving in his dishes of applewood smoked nutria and nutria fricassee. Loyola University professor Robert Thomas then organized Nutriafest, an event at which Louisiana chefs slugged it out to see who could serve the tastiest presentation of the plentiful meat: a locavore's prize.

Such an idea is not surprising coming from a state whose gastronomic ingenuity considers turtle and alligator fair game for the stew pot. Virgin toast or not, even New Orleans' Holy Trinity is edible, thanks to the city having replaced the frustratingly metaphysical Father/Son/Holy Ghost routine with the much more palatable communion of bell peppers, onions, and celery.

Confronted with an army of orange teeth, Louisiana had found a resolution that only Louisiana could deliver, a resolution that had grabbed me by my salivary glands and offered me a chance to serve my country as culinary patriot.

But not even Louisiana could deliver. The palates of restaurant patrons turned bland and trembling at the thought of eating a healthy wild animal (no growth hormones or veal cages!) that happened to come from the dishonorable rodent family, no matter how beneficial for the city and the bayou.

Sure, Cajun hunters from the nearby bayou still make home-simmered stews from freshly trapped "nutra-rats," an understandable choice for a resourceful culture that sews up turduckens and throws mudbugs into a spicy boil. (The insectile-looking mudbugs are better known as crawfish, now one of New Orleans' most renowned offerings, even though crawfish are scavengers and eat dead matter that nutria won't touch.) But a few years after the nutria promotion started, restaurants dropped it from their menus. Then the state cancelled the promotion.

Earlier in the day, I called chefs of several restaurants in New Orleans to see if they would be willing to bring back their smothered, smoked, and stuffed nutria. While the chefs enjoyed chatting about cooking invasive species as they prepared for evening service (one even shared tales of experimenting with nutria back in his culinary school days), none said yes, most of them citing the insurmountable rodent stigma. The critter non grata.

My quest then led me to a popular New Orleans cooking school (remaining anonymous at their request), where one instructor could not stop lustfully recounting her experiences with nutria tacos. "They're eating the state, so we should eat *them*. By the way, nutria is great in chili too!" she beamed while the cashier stood by in mute, lip-biting horror.

Perhaps nutria needs a marketing makeover. Like a new name. How about calling it a bayou pig? Even tour guides can get in on the fun. *Before our air-conditioned bus arrives at the dock for our swamp cruise, we'll sit down at Stinky Thibodeaux's Restaurant for his famous bayou pig étouffée. Laissez les bons temps rouler!*

As for other solutions, traps lost consideration because they were not as fast and cheap as bullets. Poison did not receive the community's approval. The prospect of releasing alligators—natural predators of nutria—into the canals similarly tanked, since alligators do not bother making a distinction between tasty nutria and tasty joggers.

Thus what might seem like a Wild West approach is the most efficient way to knock down the nutria population and spare the city from flooding. Which brings me back to the breezy pickup truck. The driver, Maurice, a superintendent of the drainage department, was scribbling out a meticulous tally of the evening's score. Since 1995, the parish's SWAT teams have bagged over 18,500 nutrias, which could have made a half million servings of chili.

Sparky and Mark's job seemed enviable: getting paid to hunt. But, alas, they had to work a regular eight-hour shift beforehand. Unlike in the wilds of the state where a hunter's only worry is inadvertently pulling a Dick Cheney on his buddy, the Jefferson Parish SWAT team is shooting in a city. With the embankment so close to homes, a scant lapse in hand-eye coordination could send a bullet into someone's living room.

Despite long days and a constant need for perfection, the team still managed to save time for smiling, all while their friends were most likely slurping down beers on Bourbon Street. When Mark's .22 jammed, Sparky announced above his spit cup, "You're an animal rights activist."

"It's easier to shoot nutria with a flashlight," Mark fired back.

Such levity seemed unusual coming from an elite duo trained to take out drug lords and hostage takers. But I found myself strangely reassured by their approach, in all its defusing humanness. It's that same untiring New Orleans spirit that returned to a flooded city three years ago and recaptured it.

The team will need the humor. "Even if we work 24/7, we can't get them all," Kerry mentioned. "They reproduce like you can't believe." Each female can start breeding at five months of age, and can crank out three litters per year, averaging five offspring per litter. They're like tribbles with appetites of Pac-Man. The nighttime shifts do provide an unrelated benefit, though: exceptional training, owing to low-light conditions, moving targets, and an urban environment. Note to aspiring drug lords: the SWAT team is a damn good shot.

As the casings filled up the pickup bed, I tried to assess my mission. I had arrived to sample nutria prepared by the inventive hands of a New Orleans chef. I was ready to eat one for the team. But I was denied a chance at culinary patriotism. Some nutria, however, would be destined for gullets, albeit not in the finest of dining settings: all spoils of the night's shift would feed the alligators at the zoo. While my visceral half—now engorged with darting curiosity and adrenaline—begged to snag one of the carcasses and stew it, I decided I didn't want to rob a caged creature of its feeding time pleasures.

So what did the neighbors think? In diligent suburban fashion, few wandered around at midnight, in naked contrast to Bourbon Street five miles away, where you're never more than a tittie beads' toss from a frozen drink machine. But with a roving sniper in the cradle of the American Dream, where were the gasping mouths? The community protests? Instead, one pedestrian barked at us, "Hey, I wanna shoot too!" while another waved a sloppy hand at us and asked, "Y'all goin' after gators?" No, just their breakfast, actually.

If the SWAT team were patrolling around any other suburban landscape in the States, the reaction would have probably been less amicable. But New Orleans' version of normalcy comes fortified with an attraction to the second amendment.

Throw in a fondness of spice rubs, and New Orleanians just might be willing to help their city by barbecuing nutria on their backyard grills after all. As long as their neighbors don't find out.

Distortion, with Injera

C all it the Bonkers quotient.

Economists have a variety of weighted indices by which to judge the financial underpinning of a neighborhood. I prefer to consider how much a neighborhood's residents spend on their pets, especially when the word daycare is used on the signage of pet grooming businesses. Such a sign greeted me a few minutes after I had emerged from the mural-lined U Street metro station in Washington, DC. For me, the storefront was a jarring but telling piece of perspective into the Washington of 2009.

The last time I had been in the capital, barely a few establishments in the neighborhood had dared to stay open. And not one was a place where your beloved Bonkers can get his rubdown by a certified canine masseuse. That was ten years ago, in 1999, when I had driven into Washington's U Street neighborhood to perform a thirty-five-minute set of punk 'n' roll. The three of us—the members of the New York City–based group Motor Betty—peeked out of the rental van windows at the eerily quiet neighborhood where we'd play our first show in our country's capital. Then we would return to the highway, as if executing a well-rehearsed guerilla maneuver. But such is the nature of road gigs.

The point of the visit, of course, was to rock out in front of whoever had heard us on DC's college radio, no matter how few fingers would end up counting the fans. Despite the time constraints of gear-humping—driving around, setting up, breaking down, and guarding musical equipment (such endeavors make up ninety percent of a gig, unless you play harmonica or spoons)—I still wanted to get a feel for our host city, the place that was willing to take a chance on an out-of-town band. As I am someone who enjoys the street-level discoveries of travel, so little foot-to-sidewalk time made me feel cheap and sullied.

I convinced my two bandmates to walk a couple of blocks from the club to U Street in search of lunch, and we found a few Ethiopian restaurants among a silent wasteland of boarded-up storefronts, a neighborhood where not even the ghosts of its bustling past cared to stir. The area was once known as Black Broadway, a place where, in the era of segregation, black Washingtonians carved out their own lively quarter with the opening of black-owned banks, nightclubs, pharmacies, hotels, and delis. A self-contained, self-reliant neighborhood. A place where squawks of Miles Davis' trumpet bounced around walls of basement clubs. Where Redd Foxx unleashed raunchy standup routines in front of patrons who wore ties.

Then the riots following the 1968 assassination of Martin Luther King, Jr., reduced much of the U Street area to a husk of rubble and empty buildings, over 1,000 of which had burned. Residents left. The stench of a rotting neighborhood attracted drug pushers, drug users, drug wars. However, what is now the largest Ethiopian community outside of Ethiopia—200,000 strong, according to the Ethiopian embassy—started to graft its roots along the moribund U Street. For fans of Ethiopian cuisine like me, probing an empty, unfamiliar street was no obstacle, as long as we stayed together.

I was close enough to smell the berbere spice wafting out of the restaurant's doors. My salivary glands started breaking down imaginary bites of tangy injera, the crepe-like sourdough bread of Ethiopia and Eritrea that also serves as utensil and plate. From the quiet, hesitant behavior of my bandmates, I knew I had to produce a good reason for us to wander into a skeleton of a neighborhood, although I began thinking that if a few restaurants chose to open there, then it can't be all that bad of a place. I countered the singer's skeptical replays of "What if it makes us sick?" (perhaps a veiled version of "Let's get the hell out of here") by telling him that in Ethiopian restaurants, you get to eat with your hands. I realized, albeit in hindsight, that my comment wasn't a decent choice of sales pitch. Outvoted and in need of sticking with the rest of my trio, I withdrew with them to the safety of bologna sandwiches or potato chips or whatever was sold at a supermarket, the only store open near the venue. And thus went our whirlwind stop in northwestern DC, apart from thirty-five minutes of entering our zone of musical expression.

What remained in my mind was a static, grotesque caricature of a city neglected. Admittedly, the thin attendance of the show, combined with my bandmates' lukewarm consideration of Ethiopian dishes such as *doro tibs* and *alecha wat*, had colored my memories of the day, contributing to such an incomplete, wanting image of my country's capital.

TEN YEARS LATER, I was peering at the doggie daycare center, the 100-year-old trim around its alcove window painted cheerful shades of purple. I kept walking along Fourteenth Street and found The Black Cat, the club where the band had played a decade earlier, surrounded by stores hawking oven mitts in the shape of Pac-Man and restaurants serving grilled octopus in chimichurri sauce. Returning to a familiar place after a long absence tends to encourage comparisons of its past and present, changing the place—in the traveler's eyes—from static to dynamic, one of the rewards of time-lapse travel.

I had arrived sans drums set, the band long since retired. I was accompanying Melanie, who was going to attend a conference in Washington for women chefs. While she would be attending seminars, I had planned on finally communicating with the U Street neighborhood by way of injera-wrapped doro tibs, boarded-up storefronts be damned.

I had difficulty finding boarded-up storefronts to damn. So I wandered down a residential side street, the moist scent of stoop-front greenery introducing freshly painted turrets of Victorian houses. Solo female joggers, ornamental cabbage, kids on Big Wheels. At the same time, a fresh layer of band stickers covered the backs of stop signs, an indication of the vitality of their indie music scene.

When I had visited the Washington of 1999, I had not yet realized that the new metro stop, the first few Ethiopian eateries, and even The Black Cat would be the sprouting seeds of the neighborhood's comeback.

I had just caught the city in the midst of an all-too-familiar urban metamorphosis. Attracted by low rents of a blighted area, scrappy artists move in; shortly after, young professionals catch a whiff of the neighborhood's nouveau coolness, arrive from other parts of the city, and begin raising rents and pushing out the very artists which gave the neighborhood the stamp of coolness in the first place. Except that in northwestern DC, at least for now, both seem to coexist side by side. I began wondering about the future of the city, about the many dynamic forces that were stretching and prodding it. Will the artists stay? Will the Ethiopian community finally receive official designation of Ninth Street as Little Ethiopia? Will the original residents of Black Broadway embrace the new neighborhood?

Back on U Street, I climbed a flight of narrow stairs of a Victorian townhouse to reach a local artist's co-op store. At the register was Josh, a young musician whose hip-hop CDs were for sale on a wall hung with framed travel photos and handmade purses. Obama paraphernalia—LP records painted over with the president's image, conveniently mountable on a wall via the spindle hole—dotted the walls.

I asked Josh about the current live music scene in DC. He wore a hopeful smile, unusual for someone ringing up purchases. "We'll be hosting live bands here on Saturday nights starting in a few weeks," he said. The space was challenging. The rooms that make up the bi-level store still have the layout of the small living rooms and bedrooms of its past life. But devoted local musicians tend to double as contortionists and should be able to make it happen.

With the store's upcoming live music in mind, I peeked out the window and imagined spying on the U Street sidewalk of fifty years ago—patrons in elegant threads emerging from a jazz club, feathered hats tipping to the ladies, blue notes and cigar smoke swirling up into the window. Slinky dresses may have given way to Nikes, but the blue notes have risen again.

Later, I would find an article from a DC newspaper in which partygoers claimed that the established Adams Morgan neighborhood, a twenty-minute walk to the northwest (and whose sidewalks host a Saturday night stiletto gridlock I had waded through the night before), no longer struck their MTV-attention-span fancies. U Street, they declared, is the next place to host the ever-moving caravan of disposable income known as trendiness.

The waves of fashion will wash past, but I believe the true spirit of a neighborhood is found in what evolves over time rather than what changes overnight. Further down U Street, I met with the hand-painted letters on the storefront of Ben's Chili Bowl that brightened the street with anachronistic swirls, preserving a wormhole to the 1950s. Yet the counterwomen twirled and snapped their fingers to the plump bass lines of Fertile Ground on the jukebox, as if serving chili-covered half-smokes was just another part of their dance. I would learn later that the Chili Bowl was one of the few establishments on U Street that remained open through both the 1968 riots and the disrupting construction of the metro stop. There must be some kind of sagacity locked up in those chili dogs.

The Ethiopian and Eritrean communities, without the need for Pac-Man oven mitts, have not only survived but thrived, their restaurants' vegetarian combinations fiery and uncharacteristically inexpensive for the area. I rounded Ninth just off U, in the center of the highest concentration of Ethiopian-run establishments, where outdoor speakers of a basement music store were energizing the sidewalk with the 6/8 cycles of Ethiopian synth-pop. As far as I can tell, The U Street neighborhood is the only place in the States where the corner convenience mart sells both gas and stacks of injera bread.

After Melanie's seminars, she and I fashioned pick-up pinchers out of injera, first at an Ethiopian restaurant, and then an Eritrean, as soccer replayed on the television and smashed lentils ended up between our fingers. Our bodies hummed with electric berbere warmth, like underground barbecue pits. Melanie was curious to experiment with Ethiopian cuisine, so we found ourselves discussing the ingredients of injera with a grocery store owner. "This brand is better, it has more teff!" the owner announced as she tapped a chubby finger onto a spongy ten-pack of injera that was baked just a few blocks away. Teff, she explained, is a tiny grain that gives the injera its distinctive tangy flavor when fermented.

Even though I found the hands-on meals sublime (almost worth trading two senators for), I realized that those experiences would become just a part, albeit an important part, of my understanding of U Street. A ten-year hunger had been appeased, and, as travel also tends to instigate, new hungers—to uncover ingredients of Ethiopian doro tibs, to uncover ingredients of the new U Street—had been hatched.

BERBERE STILL SMOLDERING in my chest, I leaned against the covered-up windows of a future tattoo parlor, claiming one of the last vacant storefronts in what used to be Black Broadway. I thought about the gig ten years before, and how insignificant I viewed it back then. Until my return to the streets of northwestern DC, I never saw how the band's brief visit could have contributed—in the same, modest way that thousands of local and visiting bands and artists have collectively contributed—to the fertile, morphing continuum that is U Street. That realization, in turn, made me feel somewhat insignificant again.

At the curb in front of me, the whitewalls of a banana-yellow 1951 Ford Victoria coasted to a noiseless stop. A college-aged man, dressed in a shrunken t-shirt and Diesel jeans, approached it in feverish pursuit. He walked in a tight, monomaniacal circle around the car and pointed the gelled wedge of his haircut—the uber-hip style that tries its best to imitate a rooster's crest—toward the open driver's side window. "Are you selling this car? Can I buy it?" asked Rooster-do.

The driver, a beefy black man whose pinstriped three-piece bulged around his chest, threw back his head and grinned. His fedora hat must have just missed grazing the roof of the Victoria. He looked as old as the car, but his face was stretchy and full of life, as if he were about to start singing. The neighborhood's past was negotiating with its present.

The driver soaked up the attention with a dreamy nod, suggesting that he had enjoyed such an encounter before. Behind the smile, he seemed to be gliding through pleasant flashbacks while the young man's offer hung in the air.

The "Hey Now" Dance

Sometimes I think that New York City's fashion paranoia was invented, at least in part, for the close quar-
ters of its subway system. With no bumpers and
brake lights to monitor during the daily commute, eyes of
subway riders are free to roam and analyze. Each subway
car is an overstuffed petri dish, each rider simultaneously a
spectator and a subject. A study in studying. And the game
gets ratcheted up with each mumbled "we're being held in
the station by the train dispatcher" announcement.

While some eyes are no doubt preoccupied with trying
to reverse-engineer the dressing process, others are busy
rolling over sartorial choices across the platform. "Thou
shalt not wear cargo pants, lest thou look like a tourist from
a fly-over state," snicker the thought bubbles above vintage
shirts and needless sunglasses.

In a wholesale failure of living up to the image of the
stylish New Yorker, I own cargo pants. But I hesitate to

wear them on the subway—not out of fear of being mistaken for a tourist, however. Sure, you might have to worry about those big, billowy pockets getting picked. But as I discovered one afternoon on the Thirty-Fourth Street F platform—in front of the ever-vigilant rush-hour audience—the New York City subway system furnishes a hazard equally as heinous as ending up with less cargo in your cargo pants: ending up with *more* cargo.

It all started when something soft bumped my ankle. Since New York City is stocked with moneyed parents who, too often enough, don't have much control over their kids, I figured a lil' one had run into me. Or maybe one of his toys rolled my way.

But when I looked down, I didn't find a kid. Or a toy. Instead, I met eye to eye with a hairy, quivering rat trying to climb up my pant leg.

I am not sure why the fight or flight reflex did not kick in right away. I wasted costly moments by reassuring myself that the tracks are the rats' domain, and the platform—four feet above the tracks—is the humans' domain, and the two should never mingle (except for occasional track work, when workers have to briefly descend into Rat World). That was a comfortable assumption I've always carried around when I would watch, with the detached curiosity of a scientist, rats scampering among the railroad ties. Like ant farms without that pesky glass. Everything along the tracks—bolts, ancient fastenings, dropped umbrellas—is covered with the same rat-colored brown grime, as if marked as *theirs*.

My denials continued. I thought that maybe the rat was trying to find its way up someone else's pant leg, and I was just watching in amazement. An out of body experience of sorts. I suppose I'd become caught up in my own spectating. In addition to the platforms serving as fashion runways, the stations occasionally offer other free channels like the Thunderbird-scented beggar, the argument between multiple personalities of the same person, and this cool new pant leg channel I just found. A sideshow for a fare. A welcome diversion away from the subway platform's never-ending battle between bleach and piss. We expect to watch the sideshow, but we think we'll never become part of it.

But, as when the tug of someone trying to wake you becomes part of your dream right before you awake, I continued to feel the undeniable tip of a snout, quaking and scheming, on my ankle.

Then I turned over another, desperate, split-second machination: maybe it was a Yorkshire terrier. When rained on, yorkies resemble rats, no matter what kinds of bows they have in their hair. Why be scared of a trembling little puppy? Maybe I should reach down and pet it.

At some point during a savage mental race down a list of species with hair—somewhere between otter and anteater, perhaps—my visceral core finally came online and I found myself employing evasive maneuvers in the form of what I call the "Hey Now" Dance. For those of you who wish to try this at home (or if you live in a public transit–free area), here's how you do it. You jump in the air, slightly kicking your legs apart, but not too far, since you don't want to injure your fellow rush-hour passengers. While looking down to make sure the rodent hasn't matched your dance steps move for move (they can navigate mazes, so why the hell not?), yell, "Hey now!" Repeat until your fellow passengers learn the dance too. Note: don't scream. You don't want to cause a stampede now, do you?

I was wondering if I should have been surprised. The underground stations remain warm year round, providing a stable nesting environment. Plenty of life-sustaining water leaks into the ever-meandering cracks in the 100-year-old subway system. Riders feed the creatures—passengers toss garbage into the tracks with customary zeal. The rats have everything they need for a comfy home. In 50,000 years, aliens, unearthing the ruins of New York's subway system, extrapolating evidence of a curious interaction between human and rodent, might even think the rat was some sort of communal mascot.

A few inevitable screams of other passengers traced the rat's escape route down the platform, or wherever it hid with that impressively compressible rib cage of his. My dancing ended in front of a young woman in a well-fitted business suit, her crossed arms to protect her personal space. I made sure to tell her that a rat tried to climb up my leg, lest she would think that I was just dancing with myself. "I know," she said with a tiny nod, a kind of minimum effort nod, her eyes aimed at some nebulous point down the tracks, "I saw it coming toward you."

I supplied her sideshow for the day, and she could not even warn me, her fellow passenger. All the while, she wore a stare that consisted of part glad-it's-not-me, part ewww-that's-nasty, and just a touch of I-know-I-look-good-in-this-suit.

As much as I could have concluded, bitterly, that she exemplified the desensitized selfishness and social withdrawal resulting from a daily melee of eight million egos, I imagined that if the rat had instead chosen to sneak up her custom-tailored business skirt, I might have been fascinated to such a degree that my words of warning might have become an inaudible puff of air. So the effect may have appeared similar—just plain staring. With the detached curiosity of a scientist, no doubt.

In spite of this sea of disconnection, I began to feel a distinct kinship with my hairy visitor from the nether reaches of the station. A score of riders watched, but only the rat made eye contact with me. He might be from a universally despised and feared species, rarely allowed into the privileged club of creatures called upon to serve as designs for stuffed, cuddly children's toys. But, like us, in the face of a crowded population, rats know how to compete. They fight over crumbs of hotdog buns; we fight over taxi rides and jobs.

Yes, like the slime that slithered from the ocean hundreds of millions of years ago, this brave rodent left the familiarity of his home (Rat World, in his case), to seek an advantage over his track-bound brethren.

And now I imagine he was just looking for a place to hide. A little chill time away from the stress of navigating around all those bipeds that can't stand the looks of him. Or he might have done so because I had waited for my lunch in front of a charcoal grill earlier that day, and to a critter whose regular diet consists of old gum wrappers and moldy pizza crusts, I must have smelled irresistible.

Sure, my dance act helped to keep him from realizing his goals. But in the end, the indifferent fate of the laundry cycle had offered me unexpected help because my indulgently comfortable but style-free cargos had not come around in the weekly rotation yet. I wore hipster-compliant blue jeans that day. Snug they were—not Robert Plant–snug, but tight enough to discourage a marginalized mammal from clawing his way to refuge. You could say I was saved by fashion.

I avoided the inconvenience of having to take my pants off on the platform, which might have been misconstrued as an entirely different kind of sideshow. I always wear presentable underwear, though, just in case. That's my own New York fashion tip.

Buns and Bile

It was a cultural ambush on home turf. Rarely have I felt as curiously foreign as when I was immersed in an adrenaline-fired encounter in my own country: a glimpse into the headband-wearing world of competitive eating.

The choice of location heightened the effect. The third annual Choo Choo's Hamburger Eating Contest went down under the familiar shade of an elevated subway stop just minutes from my home in Astoria, New York.

Even more ominous, the event appeared as the antithesis of Astoria's standard gastronomy, one of Greek restaurants and their patrons chatting and enjoying each other's company during family dinnertime; Italian-American bakeries run by three generations, all behind the counter simultaneously; Colombian restaurants in no rush to either serve orders of *bistec a caballo* or flip booths. For Astoria—a landmark-free, lightly-touristed neighborhood just across the river from the compressed fury of Manhattan—a meal is a celebration, a pleasure, a gathering. The only food-based competition I could imagine would be to discover which restaurant serves the tenderest octopus or the crispiest, flame-grilled whole branzino.

Such pursuit of enjoyment has no place in an event that, while also centered on eating, claims a purpose of neither pleasure nor nutritional procurement. When I stepped sideways into Choo Choo's restaurant, I almost ended up pinned between a television crew and a wall of burgers stockpiled in neat rows like ammunition. Somewhere from within a cluster of competitors and reporters, stray comments like "I ran in the morning to make sure I'd be hungry" and "I hope we get lots of water" danced above the crackling hiss of beef meeting fire. Where did these bun-dipping soldiers come from and what did they want?

I knew I should not allow myself to become too surprised at the substantial glutting of one's digestive tract in a set timeframe. After all, America is the country that invented such advanced, efficiency-minded, caloric delivery methods as fast food, the TV dinner (atop its equally American accomplice, the TV tray), lunch *al desko*, and the ubiquitous four words that systematically lower the emphasis on quality while raising the average waistband size: All You Can Eat.

The day's contest demonstrates that even Queens, America's most diverse county—where more than half of the population was born outside the States—can assimilate.

Bobbing in the back of the restaurant's six-table dining area, the inescapable girth of last year's champion, Brooklyn native Will "The Champ" Millender, loomed like a bull in a holding pen. As he posed, grimly game-faced, for pictures with his trophy belt, I asked him if he trained for the event. "No," he answered in a flat syllable. "But for longer competitions, I might do some water training." For the benefit of the casual, non-competitive eater, water training is the practice of filling up one's stomach with water to stretch it out.

Will had still been savoring his success at a recent contest in the formidable milkshake-drinking discipline. "The strawberry-eating contest," he boasted, "was later on the same day."

Standing across from me, Joel "The Cannon" Podelsky, his headband poised for action, pointed to Will and added, "Strawberries were the only contest where I beat you." (Joel would later go on to devour a pumpkin pie in seventy seconds on *America's Got Talent*, earning him three buzzes and crotchety scorn from British judge Piers Morgan.) When I asked them if they had any predictions, Joel, with the seriousness of an Olympic skier interviewed by a major network, remarked, "Will is the favorite. But you never know. Some new guy could come in."

The sound engineer, in mid-knob-tweak, asked me if I was one of the competitors. After I told him that I just wanted to watch, he asked, "Why don't you enter? Think of it as a free lunch. Just stuff your face."

The thought of a free lunch did sound appealing, especially in the middle of a recession. In the next moment, Choo Choo's steam tables and bins of condiments—hallmarks of meals built for speed—shook loose a recollection within me, a reality from which I can never hide. My parents told me that before I was born, they often used to pick up subs at the first Subway sandwich shop ever opened, in Bridgeport, Connecticut—the one that seeded the thousands of other Subway sandwich shops around the planet.

And perhaps seeded me too. Instances of the franchise keep peeking out of just about every landscape in my national and international travels, as if following me, waiting for me to admit that no matter how many bouillabaisses and shrimp *al ajillos* with which I indulge my palate, my DNA owes its helixes to salty, cold-cut-flavored amniotic fluid, some sort of distinguished, all-American watermark I should be proud of.

Even if I had been harboring such demons all this time, how could I justify entering an eating contest? "It goes against everything the Slow Food movement is about," Melanie, a member of Slow Food USA, had told me before I left for Choo Choo's. A compelling point. Slow Foodies advocate, among other agricultural and gastronomic ideas, eating for flavor and enjoyment rather than treating eating as a mechanical act that needs to be streamlined. So why, then, would *anyone* want to enter an eating contest? Are they preparing for a hideous, apocalyptic future of brutal food shortages and every man for himself? Do they seek an eater's high?

To find out, I signed the waiver and would appear in the second heat.

"CHOO! CHOO!"—or maybe it was "Chew! Chew!"—barked the thicket of spectators, blocking the sidewalk in front of the restaurant. A babbling drunk, dragging around a bottle of forty-ounce beer covered in a paper bag, floated in and out of the crowd, providing more amusement than the first heat, a row of seven chummy men who tapped each other with amused elbow nudges as if they were on their lunch break. In the five-minute time limit, some of them could not even down more than one of the four-ounce burgers. Cheers grew sour and warped. The winner of the heat managed three, but not for long, because he sprinted to the next storefront to obey the urgent disquiet of his digestive tract and jettisoned his lead onto defenseless concrete. A "reversal of fortune," in competitive eating parlance.

Even my untrained jaws could do better, I thought as I seated myself in a row of nine competitors of the next heat. Tally boards behind us, geometric stacks of meat and bun hemming us in, a naïve rumble of hunger groped around my stomach with its acidic paws. Just as a bicycle is stripped of its nonessential weight to make it race-ready, the burgers before me were bare. Not a dab of mayo, not a single confetti-shred of lettuce. Bacon was out of the question. I turned over the thought of asking for a few tomato slices.

No time for that. The crowd demanded entertainment. Peaceful weekend errand-runners in t-shirts and flip-flops had transmogrified into a chanting throng at the sight of a spectacle. I think I recognized one of the women as a neighbor who shops at the same grocery store as me. But I never recalled seeing her stare so intently at a container of low-fat yogurt as she was staring at us.

The onlookers yelled the countdown into our faces, ending in a piercing "go!"—thus launching the gastronomic sprint often criticized as a waste of food; as reckless self-endangerment; as a poor role model; as a perversion of cuisine. I wondered why the same critics didn't bother objecting to other American sporting events, like the Daytona 500, a contest whose copious use of fossil fuel makes oil barons nod and chuckle; presents its contestants an ever-present threat of a gruesome death; and may encourage spectators to drive fast. And entrants don't actually reach any destination, since they are literally driving in circles. To avoid being hypocritical, we might as well ban all competitions, except maybe checkers.

But checkers never seems to trigger the flood of adrenaline that only a sort-out-the-pecking-order competition can provide. First burger down.

Funny thing, that adrenaline, how it simplifies sensory input. It shuts down unnecessary mental noodling and throbs with a beastlike, fight-or-flight ugliness. Through the time-warp ether of adrenaline, I thought I heard chants of hip-hop wafting from the deejay rig. Echoes of shouts without the shouts themselves. I could see the appeal of such a dreamy bolt to the finish line.

One base sensation, however, refused to be silenced, and grew sharper and more eager as the others laid low: taste. If I ate any faster, I would not be chewing, and hence would not taste anything flame broiled. That was the threshold that had to be crossed to seize the spoils of victory, a threshold too undesirable for me to approach. If I harbored layers of fast food protoplasm, I'm sure they had recoiled in horror. An eater's high? Didn't happen for me.

With my final score of three burgers, the most I could have eaten while still tasting them along the way, I would have won the first heat, had I been in it. But an unknown contestant at the other end of the table of my heat finished off eight of the four-ounce burgers, making me look like a mere control subject. Joel, waiting for his seat in the third and final heat, undoubtedly contemplating his earlier prediction, leaned into me and said, "That's gonna put some heat on us." That was heat that the spectators would not notice, thanks to the distraction provided by the free un-eaten burgers that the Choo Choo's staff passed around.

Will took his place at the end of the table, standing in-stead of sitting, holding court with his sun-blocking silhou-ette. With a shaved head and unbroken stare, his presence could have intimidated any competitor, except Joel, who was engrossed in separating and rearranging buns and pat-ties on his plate like playing edible solitaire. The booms and pops of the deejay's drum-heavy selection jolted the final heat of seven into a not-so-synchronized ballet of dunking, shoving and cheek-bulging. Nodding with the groove, Will didn't seem burdened by that pesky taste-the-food hang-up. Tasting the food was for amateurs like me. For the compet-itive eater, food is a piece of sports equipment.

And so was sitting down. Earlier, Joel had enlightened me with the fact that standing elongates the digestive sys-tem and makes more room for more match-time action. After four burgers had disappeared into his mouth, Will hopped like a boxer, another technique for moving food down the plumbing. They weren't eating the burgers; they were eradicating them. Bizarre, aggressive...and somehow both disturbing and captivating. They managed to ex-change the relaxing enjoyment of flavor for the invigorat-ing enjoyment of competition, demonstrating what the thrill of victory could drive humankind to do.

In the midst of such unabashed table manners, I looked up at the elevated N station overhead, its wrought iron flourishes not having changed in eighty years, reminding me of the borough's restaurant culture and its contrast with what was transpiring in front of me. My eyes became sway-ing film cameras and the scene was about to accelerate into a spray of wet bun debris without the benefit of a slow-motion climax.

While Joel's ingredient shuffling scored him five burgers in five minutes, Will and his power hopping dominated the round with eight. Thus the crowd, now treated with its third course of free burgers, had just witnessed a first in Choo Choo's history: a tie, forcing a sudden death, two-burger scarf-off.

Matching Will's bulk pound for pound, a grinning, red-cheeked Richard McLeon, a transplant from New Mexico who had won my heat in his first-ever eating competition, ignored the hollers and arm thrusts and mirrored Will's cool command of oral machinery, down to the last crumb. The winner? Richard by a bite. Soon after, he found himself in a flurry of photo ops with the trophy—topped with a winged athlete, like one you'd encounter at a track meet or wresting championship. Does that qualify competitive eating as a sport? Just ask the spectators. What would any sport be without them?

In between camera flashes, I asked the twenty-six-year-old champion what he would do with his cash prize. Richard seemed unprepared for the question. "Put it in savings," he finally said, maintaining a stress-free smirk. Since he notched such an impressive start to his competitive eating career with humility and recession-time economic acumen, I imagined what Richard could accomplish after training. Soon we might find him bankrupting a Las Vegas buffet restaurant in one visit (unless, of course, the hotel does the Vegas thing and charges all gawkers for admission).

I left knowing I'd never have the talent or the mindset for joining the ranks of Will and Richard. I walked up the stairs of the N train's elevated platform and, as if to realign my stomach with Astoria (or was it to apologize to Astoria?), I found myself already planning my next meal, a leisurely repast of dry white wine and fish with crispy skin.

Pedaling for Agrotourism

The clarity was painful. We had landed in a curious parallel universe where a blackberry is something sweet you eat off of a mound of whipped cream, as opposed to something plastic, nervously clutched and pampered, to score an antisocial high.

But before we could begin a hunt for such ripe edibles, our lesson continued. "You have to communicate," a fatherly voice announced from behind us. I was balanced on the front of a tandem bicycle parked next to a bike shop on Île d'Orléans, a farm-blanketed island in Quebec's St. Lawrence River, as the owner of the shop was giving Melanie and me a lesson on the basics of tandem riding. Melanie, who had never learned how to ride a bike (and never had a need for one while growing up in New York City), waited on the back seat of the tandem, and was either absorbing the tutorial or wondering how I had convinced her to join me on a vehicle so alien to her.

The bike felt somewhat unfamiliar to me as well, since I had never attempted to ride a tandem before. "If you are going to stop or make a turn," the bike shop owner continued, "you should let her know."

As I listened, I found myself thumbing dual gear changers while envisioning the impending deluge of cassis liqueur and maple-syrup ham and all the grilled organic asparagus I could metabolize. While travelers have long been familiar with ecotourism and medical tourism, Île d'Orléans appeals to curious visitors with agrotourism.

Unfortunately, agrotourism doesn't have the recognition it deserves. Since it lacks zip-line rides and photo-ops with loin-clothed natives, agrotourism might be imagined as an outing to watch some fuzzy stalks shake in the breeze, and then the afternoon gets a shade more exciting when you happen to catch a nearby cow taking a leak. "Yup! That's where your food comes from," the guide will announce like a game-show host as he wipes sweat off his forehead with his sleeve. "Now c'mon, everybody, let's go pick aphids off of tomato plants!"

At least for Île d'Orléans, agrotourism translates into how you can taste the harvests close to where they were grown, often at the farms themselves. Bakeries, cheesemakers, a brewery, and endless rows of rhubarb nuzzle up to grazing lamb, chicken, and geese. Twenty-nine varieties of apples grow on the fifty-square mile island, preserving genetic diversity of our food supply and offering a lavish choice of flavors to boot.

But the island's most recognized offerings are its wines and liqueurs. The fermentation of fruit juice on the island is not the product of a trend to satisfy a recent foodie fever, though. The island has been bringing the Quebecois to drunken bliss for centuries, ever since the French explorer Jacques Cartier initially dubbed the place "Isle of Bacchus" because of all the wild grapevines he saw crawling over the island when he arrived in the early 1500s.

After considering the island's restaurants that employ locally grown ingredients, I suppose the island could be pimping gastrotourism as well. After all, the farmers of the island don't just grow crops—they also love to cook. In 2006, they documented their passions by publishing a bilingual cookbook titled *Île d'Orléans: Farmers in Chef Hats*.

And that's why I chose the bicycle. I wanted to travel at a pace leisurely enough to allow us to draw in the same tactile blessings that the farmers enjoy—soaking in the vistas of the crops overlooking the St. Lawrence, all while smelling the busybody trail of cross-pollination in the June air. The same sun that would coax a red currant into ripening would be the same sun that would draw my sweat. A hermetically sealed SUV just wouldn't do.

"But I don't know how to balance myself on a bike," Melanie protested.

"In the back seat, all you have to do is pedal," said I, the biker who had never ridden in a tandem before. And by our first incline, I began to realize that I might have oversimplified the required technique. Having not biked for a few years, I figured I was out of practice. But that theory did not explain the new sensation of someone seemingly pulling the bike from behind. The direction of the pulling became more erratic, as if I were fighting invisible challengers in a contest to remain king of the mountain. I began to wonder whether she was pedaling backward or forward.

At some point, my legs decided to turn to sponge. I failed to take notice of that important development because I was still focusing on our first goal of the day: lunch at a *cabane à sucre*—a sugar shack—the party-time institution of the Quebecois that delivers traditional meals to keep families warm in the winter and happy in the summer.

Then mind and matter met again, an inevitable rendez-vous, perhaps triggered when I asked Melanie how she was doing on the back seat, perhaps by my sudden inability to pedal. We decided we should take a break. Stopping was the easy part. As soon as we did, however, the phantom jostlers yanked us right down into an open field of fuzzy stalks shaking in the breeze. As we sat on the soil, the tandem on top of us, I began to see the appeal of a low-octane outing such as, say, picking aphids off of tomato plants.

Thick, chewy clouds paused above the river and waited with us. Or perhaps for us. Even the wind, which had been insistent and impatient, halted, as if to offer us neophytes a grace period. We took it.

We arrived late for our lunch reservation, but the sugar shack was in no danger of running out of food. Or music. A dining hall as wide as an aircraft hangar swallowed us into its belly swirling with dancing schoolchildren, the occasional note from an accordion somewhere in the center sneaking over the children's giggles. For me, booty shaking was not a realistic objective, since my legs refused to do anything more than hang under the table like imbeciles.

But they were not required to tuck into the feast placed before us. A steaming meat pie, pea soup, a crunchy cabbage salad, and maple syrup-glazed ham crowded the table, with more plates of salads and vegetables too far to reach. They all framed a central bowl of fried, twisted pork cracklings. The Quebecois must view themselves as astute Catholics because when they heard that Jesus equivocated his body and blood to bread and wine, the Quebecois took the next step and decided that something as rich and lobe-like as pork cracklings must be called *oreilles de crisse*—ears of Christ.

If you've never eaten a juicy *tourtière*—a pork and beef pie spiced with spices such as cinnamon and cloves—I can best describe it as what you like about dinner wrapped up in what you like about dessert. The dinner-dessert effect is amplified by a traditional dollop of fruit ketchup, a condiment both sweet and savory. This is the kind of chow that keeps the Quebecois alive and singing in the winter when the air threatens to give them frostbite if they take too long to pee outside. Even my French-Canadian grandmother, who had served me my first meat pie, would have been impressed.

Even though ham cooked in maple syrup seems almost redundant next to a pie whose filling is half pork, the ham recalled what ham can—and should—achieve. Instead of a dry, salty lump resembling ground up tires dyed pink—as is the case with most supermarket hams in the States—the sugar shack's thick-sliced ham managed to deliver tenderness without making you feel like you've just repeatedly licked a block of salt.

My legs began to throb again with life. While undisclosed quantities of ham and peas weighed our torsos down, adding more ballast to our ride, I figured it was a prudent time to consider why the bike was dragging so much. A search through my backpack reminded me of how randomly we had packed when we left Quebec City earlier that morning, placing whatever didn't fit in our luggage into the backpack. I reached in and found what we had forgotten to remove from the backpack this morning: Melanie's 800-watt hair dryer. Then I probed deeper into the bag and found six large jars of jam.

I felt a pirate-like need to lighten our load and throw something overboard. Made at small, organic farms from Quebec, the jams were too special to chuck. Could I sneak the hair dryer into a passing mailbox without Melanie noticing? I even insisted on paying for lunch with a pile of one- and two-dollar coins instead of bills, as I clung to a warped hope that shaving off a few ounces of metal from our pockets might even matter.

What would end up saving the hair dryer? The twenty-mile-per-hour tailwind. And a downhill stretch. As we pedaled to the westernmost point of the island, the wind at our backs allowed us to slurp up the views of centuries-old clapboard houses. White-trimmed barns looked ready to live in. "It's like Little House on the Prairie," Melanie gloated as we swished past marching rows of grapevines, the soaring Montmorency waterfall on the northern bank of the river always visible, as if it were following us. We barely noticed when a thick procession of manure trucks forced us into the two-foot-wide shoulder of the road where we had to slow down and run over drain grates.

I tried to enjoy the cassis sorbet we ordered at the Chocolaterie de l'Île d'Orléans, at the western tip of the island, where we met with a silent, gauzy view of Quebec City's petite skyline three miles upriver. But such an intimate waterline view only meant that the return trip would be entirely uphill. And the wind was no longer our friend, since now we had to slap it head-on.

Our glutes began expressing their discontent with the unyielding bike seats. Each time we were forced into a pothole, the seats spit dual geysers of venom into our skeletons. I did not dare to stand up on the pedals, lest our ganglier center of gravity attract our invisible shoving playmates. But there were wines to sample, so we low-geared it into the nearest winery, St. Pétronille, where the owner poured us a rosé dry enough to earn a coveted spot on the rear-wheel rack despite its weight. Out of deference to our backsides, we stood for the tasting.

The previous week, in Quebec City, we had enjoyed produce that more often than not had been brought in from the island. Thus, even before we had arrived on the island, her farmers had demonstrated that crops grown for flavor instead of size and shelf life are the rule, not special-interest exceptions. Now that we met the island, touched it, drank it, we noticed how refreshingly far the island went to preserve its *joie de vivre*. Most other landscapes so close to a large North American city tend to fall prey to the highest bidder, who then endeavors to build the cheapest, ugliest condos fathomable. But on Île d'Orléans, the farmers—and a few lucky residents in houses passed down through generations—still have the best view, from under their chef hats, of course.

I gazed over the grapevines that wrapped their way to the island's northern ridge overlooking the river. From this distance, the waterfall seemed frozen yet still imposing, even when framed beneath the massive waves of the mainland's Laurentian Mountains. The farmers live in a bustle of photosynthesis, yet they can just as easily dust off their pants and leap over to Quebec City, where they can raise their beers to a punk rock show or nap on the city's old fortification wall or get a badass tattoo or buy funky European boots. Or see how much their farm's fruit ketchup has been marked up in the grocery stores.

All the more reason to explore in a vehicle with a negligible carbon footprint, I kept saying to myself. What a shame that the headwind did not share my passion.

The owner of the bed and breakfast where we were staying also doubled as the island's only cab driver. Such convenience of which helped Melanie spawn an idea: "Can't we have him pick us up and tie the bike to the roof?"

I felt a reliance on a combustion engine would deflate the purpose, poison our fragile and fleeting oneness with the land. I refused to be upstaged by unchecked breezes and a few jars of jam, and I somehow persuaded Melanie to pedal with me to our last stop, a fruit farm, and back to the rental shop.

With so many farms, we failed to find the right one. The only sign I remember was a curious warning displaying figure of a child lying on her back in a sort of comfy lounging position. It read

WATCH OUT FOR OUR CHILDREN
THEY COULD BE YOURS

Some municipalities have issues with bored youth, such as vandalism and petty crime. Île d'Orléans appears to be encumbered with the special problem of children sleeping in the road. There was no time to ponder the sign's meaning further, as we needed to keep cranking the pedals to avoid losing the little momentum we had earned as we yearned to reach the top of the hill.

And we made it. So there we were, surrounded by the fertility of the island, the wind spreading pollen in a firestorm of spores, the unseasonably toasty sunshine fueling our elation. This is what I originally had hoped for, I said to myself, as I flicked my eyes over my sunburned forearms, sweat having carried off their coating of sunscreen many potholes ago. We'd visited barely half of the farms and wineries we had intended to. But crossing the top of the island's spine changed our fortune. We began to glide downhill to the victorious music of flapping air and Doppler-shifted bird songs. And no sleeping children in our path. A patch of rare new pavement even awaited us far off at the bottom of the hill.

It waited for us all right. I never knew how fresh, smooth pavement could be so cruel because I spotted the outline of a hole in the old asphalt just before the start of the patch. As we smacked the air and approached, I noticed that it wasn't a pothole in front of us, but a whole family of them, scattered across the entire shoulder.

I could not swerve into the car lane because it was currently owned by a truck rumbling by with its multi-ton payload of asparagus or wild gooseberries or cow shit. I knew the pothole family was our next stop. I began braking, killing most of that juicy, elusive, coquettish momentum. But I couldn't stop it all. It was the one occasion all day when I wished we had no momentum, no ballast of jam jars. Where was that ornery headwind when you needed it?

I picked what seemed to be the smallest crater. The impact made a deceptively brief rattle, but its effects were predictable. We pulled over and wobbled our battered derrieres off the tandem. We could not have been a mile from the rental shop, but Melanie, who had never sat on a hard bike seat before this day, made it clear that our ride was finished. I realized I should have warned her I was braking, just as the shop owner had recommended. Melanie pointed to a bed and breakfast across the street and said she needed a drink.

An SUV drove into the parking lot. The driver popped his head out and asked, "You biked in *this* wind?" Only a fellow cyclist would ask such questions. I believe they knew the answer already. They had racked their bikes on the bumper of their SUV and told us they hadn't been tempted to remove them all day.

Inside the bed and breakfast, the host who spun his palms together and greeted us in English was not only the man who would usher us to a table, he was also the chef and the owner of the establishment, Le Canard Huppé. Phillippe Rae was also the culinary consultant of *Farmers with Chef Hats*.

"I think the restaurant put that pothole there to make us stop," Melanie commented to me. She found a seat—padded, of course—and clutched a cocktail, while I returned the bike to the shop. When I rode the bike a quaint three minutes further down the road to the shop, the proximity began to suggest such a convenient ploy.

But I doubt Chef Phillippe had time to swing a pick and sabotage an already neglected road. When I walked back to the restaurant, I saw our table had become a jukebox spinning Phillippe's greatest hits—shrimp crème brûlée with cheese from the island; scallop ceviche with ruby-red tomatoes and mint; and a carnivorous triumvirate of deer, wild boar, and caribou filets. Eating the edible flowers that garnished each dish gave us the vaguely liberating thrill of feeling like we were grazing animals—completing a perverse dance all around the food chain, pleasing both the simplest and most advanced parts of our brainstems. If Phillippe had actually managed to dig up the pavement in between broiling cheese and reducing sauces, I should thank him.

I began to see the parallels between a tandem bike and a relationship. You ride together, you crash together. But without both people working at it, the bike won't get very far.

WE CALLED THE ISLAND'S ONLY CAB DRIVER to pick us up at the restaurant. Since the cabbie, Stephane, and his wife had emigrated from France, we discussed the differences between his country of birth and Quebec. "The French of Quebec is 'Old French,'" he mentioned. He continued with a comment about my limited French ("It's not bad—for an American"), to which I replied, "All the French I know I learned from subtitles, the Internet, and Serge Gainsbourg lyrics," which was the truth.

On our way back to Quebec City the next morning, Stephane dropped us off at a few of the wineries we could not visit the day before. A proprietor of the vineyard Isle de Bacchus hurried into her tasting room, wiping topsoil off her hands as she greeted us ("Sorry, I was just planting a few flowers") before pouring us samples of her award-winning ice wine. In low-rider jeans, appearing ready to boogie down at a Quebec City hotspot, a fifth-generation cassis grower from the farm Cassis Monna & Filles, a mile down the road, walked us into her tasting room, all while her nimble passion for cassis and its many culinary uses (in salad dressings, cookies, sauces for pork and game) proved that the dance floors of the city would have to wait.

The jams—having traveled enough around the island to become agrotourists themselves—all survived. The cloudberry jam is nearly irreplaceable, since I've hardly found anyone in the States who even knows what cloudberries are. One acquaintance I'd spoken with thought they must be the next generation of handheld electronic devices. Comments like that make me want to hop on a bike loaded down with a crate of jam while I suck in parsnip pollen, and split the wind the way Île d'Orléans splits the St. Lawrence.

Dispatching Shellfish and Getting Engaged

As I clutched a box of frozen meat pies, I said to myself, This could be the break I was looking for.

The frozen food aisle is not usually part of my habit trail. But after arriving in Percé, a coastal Quebecois town, months after the high tourist season had ended, I surmised the only route to a hot meal started and ended in the town's only grocery store. With all the town's haute cuisine restaurants closed for the winter, I could imagine what I had missed—seared scallops drizzled with a ground cherry reduction, or maybe medallions of caribou on a bed of ice-wine-spiked arctic snow.

But heating up the *tourtières*—Quebecois meat pies—at 350 degrees for half an hour has its unexpected perks. Since I was compelled to reckon with the tourtières (four for only $3.99!), that meant the now-drowsy coastal town was no longer busy entertaining thousands of fanny-packed tourists. Whale-watching boats had been dry-docked. Scores of summer workers folding all those fluffy towels had long since left, along with hundreds of the town's own snowbirds. By early November, less than one hundred Clamato-chugging villagers hunkered down to keep the coast from being invaded by packs of unruly harbor seals.

What remained was a town that had shorn its theme-park veneer and prepared for hibernation, its yellow and red Legoland houses sticking up from an almost treeless landscape. This was the real Percé. Or at least that was what I kept telling Melanie when she asked me why I wanted us to go to such a chilly locale during its off season. For years, we have predicated entire travel itineraries on what new gastronomic paths we could explore. This time, I had brought her to a place when its culinary offerings seemed limited to what prepared food could be thawed and heated.

But there was something else open. Something that never winters and cannot hide. Rocher Percé, an imposing landmark of vertical rock, looms just off the coast of the town, and thanks to its handsomely peculiar geography, the rock is synonymous with the town itself. I planned to make the rock my partner in Operation *Coucher de Soleil* (Operation Sunset), to be performed for Melanie. But she didn't know that yet.

In the meantime, allow me to introduce my accomplice: an island that is all cliff and almost no turf, is as tall (and vertical) as New York's twenty-two-story Flatiron Building, and cuts over a quarter mile into the Gulf of Saint Lawrence. From the north, the limestone island, with an arch underneath one end, invokes images of a grazing horse, confident and freakishly tall. From the south, the rock takes on the shape of a Scottish terrier with its snout busy in a dog bowl. From every angle, though, Rocher Percé dwarfs the mainland and makes one feel like a speck of moss. It's Canada's Gibraltar, but with seals instead of monkeys.

Before we could commence the operation, the images of big-boned animals chowing down were making us hungry, which brings me to my next rationalization—I mean advantage—of raiding the frozen food aisle. We have dined at some of the province's best restaurants, but what better way is there to understand the underpinnings of a culture's native cuisine than to sample their ready-made fare, the weakest link?

We were surprised that the tourtières, filled with pork, beef, and potato, and seasoned with cloves, came close to resembling some bakery-fresh tourtières we've eaten in Quebec City. It's a good thing they were satisfying because we were prepared to eat box after box of them for the next three days, along with a tub of lobster spread and some of Percé's own smoked salmon we found at the grocery store. Richard, the owner of our bed and breakfast, noticed our predicament and offered to drive us to a year-round fishmonger in the next town the following morning. We were his only guests that week.

What a thoughtful and merciful gesture. But when the morning arrived, so did the remnants of a hurricane that doused the town with the worst storm the remaining residents—all sixty-eight or so of them—had seen in their lifetimes. This did not bode well for our trip to the fish market. Or for the basements of coastal homes.

We looked out our window ("double room with view of the Rock") and noticed that the Rock had disappeared somewhere in the soupy grayness of the storm. This did not bode well for Operation Coucher de Soleil.

From the window, the out-of-scale waves thrashing over the town pier in slow motion seemed like a poorly executed cinematic special effect. I half-expected a gilled, biped monster to step onto shore while the residents, all suddenly Japanese, scream phrases like "Repent!" in badly dubbed English. Route 132, Percé's main (and only) drag, was now a river. The toilet would not flush anymore. I didn't care for the morning's special effects. Why don't we just put on the lights and—

Nothing. The power had been knocked out. Better tell Richard.

I didn't find him downstairs, but I found the pump he had set up to suck out a foot of water from the basement. I began making a mental count of the remaining tourtières in the freezer and the remaining days we had left in Percé, and then did a variety of fractional math. Small fractions. Meanwhile, deep in my luggage, a little square box holding a ring with an ornate combination of white gold, platinum, and cut stones was snorting "now you're officially a classy guy!" but Melanie could not hear it, luckily.

THE RED SURF proved to be the most curious consequence of the storm. Unending rows of angry, bloody water slapped up against the coast. Now that the sun began to poke holes in the clouds, we saw how the rainwater gushing down the more than 300-meter peaks to the west of town had sent brick-colored sediment into the Gulf by way of everyone's basement. As fast as the storm had come, it fled, as if it were embarrassed to have attacked such a charming little town.

With his basement pumped dry, Richard dodged fallen tree branches and flooded roadsides en route to the town of Sainte-Thérèse-de-Gaspé, driving us on his promised trip to the fish market.

They're open? On a Sunday? After the worst storm the peninsula had seen in a lifetime? In a place where grocery stores practically devote an entire aisle to Clamato, it's clear that the folks of Percé and the rest of the surrounding Gaspé Peninsula consider seafood a pillar in their quality of life. I should have guessed such a level of devotion from a coast used as a fishing center for centuries, first by the native Mi'kmaq nation and then by French settlers. We exited the market with a pair of gangly New Brunswick lobsters and a bag of local mussels that the store had been showering with a constant stream of water to keep them wet, fresh, and sand-free—a venerable spa for mollusks.

The sky opened up with a deep, healing blue that one only sees right after storms, intensifying the pink and red roofs of the Peninsula. The box in my pocket could not produce a snappy comeback now. After all, despite a few dozen pumps gurgling, the town had survived the storm, and its instinct to bounce back had already kicked in, as it had when a storm three decades ago took the pier with it.

Such an instinct returned me to Operation Coucher de Soleil. After a lunch of emu terrine and spiced cauliflower (perhaps the intrepid seafood market should rename itself to "Not Just Seafood"), I made a solo dry run up to the end of the cliff-skirted peninsula, right across from Rocher Percé. It was deserted. Not even a seal frolicked below.

As the close-up view of the Rock is a reliable tourist attraction, a small booth, listing a suggested donation, stood just below the last ascent up to the edge of the continent. Not surprisingly, none of the sixty-eight residents was willing to work the booth in November. I imagined that if I had left a five-dollar bill on the windowsill, a bird would probably grab it, shred it up, and turn it into a nest.

Having found a most suitable level of desertion, I returned to the B & B and brought a reluctant Melanie back up to the chilly lookout point. To watch the *coucher de soleil*—sunset—of course. Across the strait, the Rock's pointy forehead towered over us, peaceful and disarmed, as if the island were a vessel that had run aground. On the other side below us, the white-trim houses of Percé lay scattered around the coast, far enough away so that we no longer heard the buzzing of water pumps.

Bilingual signs warned us to refrain from wandering close to the edge. They were friendly reminders that the cliffs have achieved their dramatic vertical stature because chunks of them periodically fall off, and have been doing this at least since woolly mammoths were the barbecued flavor of the month. Nothing like a little danger to heighten the beauty.

The wind began to play a game where it made me feel daft that my species' evolution doesn't currently include a coating of fur. The taunting backfired because it made us huddle together—something fortuitous for the operation, after all. Melanie, still thinking that I just wanted her to enjoy the view while we slowly froze, was shooting me the "I can't believe what I do for you" look. I'd say that look was about two thirds patience and one third annoyed. But I knew that the threshold between good humor and teeth-chattering irritability could be a gust away. I had to act.

Thankfully, a few clouds finally began to catch fire from the ducking sun. I removed the box from my pocket and opened it, exposing the diamond and sapphire engagement ring to the tangerine-streaked sky. "If the sunset isn't spectacular enough for you, here's something shiny I found in the shrubs," I said to Melanie. With no vegetation taller than our kneecaps protecting us, the wind was having its way, daring our lips to stay red. But they did.

Because she said yes.

I OPENED THE SAUCEPAN LID. Puffs of sweet, lobster-scented steam billowed out. Following the scent to his kitchen, Richard, in his ultra-basic English, asked me for my recipe. I answered in my ultra-basic French, which includes mimes of varying understandability, especially after a few glasses of wine. Flip the lobster over and cut him in half (mime: I moved my hand from my forehead to my abdomen). While *vivant* (live)? Yes, while vivant (I flailed my hands like claws). Clean him and smear with a mixture of white wine, slightly fried garlic, salt, and olive oil on inside of meat (I rubbed my belly). Sauté in a pan (the word sauté is conveniently French).

It would seem that more people would prefer to celebrate an engagement by being served dinner, or at least dessert, in an atmosphere of linen tablecloths and an internationally informed deejay spinning sensual world music. And then there's Melanie and me, who preferred celebrating by killing and cooking our own dinner, sans linen table-cloths, sans deejay. It's a reflection of where our passions lie, of how, over the years, we have connected so well in the probing of gastronomy's depths. (To preserve the romantic effect, I'll ignore the fact that Percé made the choice for us, since no restaurants in town were open, with or without deejays).

With eight-inch knife in hand, I reflected that anyone who enjoys shellfish could benefit from killing a lobster, at some time or another. Not because it's enjoyable, which it is not. It underscores the cycle of life of which we are a part. The action makes you more cognizant of what you are taking away so that you can have a sublime meal. I often wonder how many more animals would be roaming the planet—cage-free—if every person had to kill his or her own dinner, at least once in a while.

Dispatching mussels is less dramatic—just put the lid on them—but it makes you appreciate them no less. Even so, the mussels proved to be some of the puffiest and freshest we've ever eaten. They tasted as if they had spent their entire lives in a sea of duck fat. I decided that the next time we cook mussels, I should first put them under one of those tabletop feng shui or yin yang or now-with-more-chi-energy waterfalls to emulate what the fishmonger did. Then I'll steam the mussels just as they've reached their yoga highs.

The lobster provided an unrepentantly cholesterol-laden climax of our celebratory meal. As a bonus, we had agreed that the tail meat wasn't overcooked, nor was the claw meat undercooked, which showcased the sweetness of the lobsters. Melanie and I tend to talk about cooking in the hopelessly obsessed way a jazz musician might talk about how seductively a guitarist plays a minor seventh chord, or how a great drum solo carries the melody of a song. "I think I balanced out the cooking of the claws and the tails right, if I can say so myself," I mentioned to Melanie.

"You did a lot of things right today," she answered.

RICHARD RETURNED THE RECIPE-SHARING FAVOR by listing the ingredients to the classic Quebecois dish *cretons* when he served it to us the following morning. Cretons, molded blocks of ground pork and spices, seemed perversely familiar to me. That is because they are like meat pies without the crust, and because of that similarity, I could not shake the image of a timid creature that had just shed its protective shell, and I almost felt guilty eating it. Almost.

FROM THE AIR, a skinny strip of greenness—could be scrub, could be moss—came into view along the top of Rocher Percé, emphasizing the perplexingly improbable thinness of the rock.

The Saint Lawrence River and its namesake gulf run the theme of cliff-studded terrain from Quebec City, whose fortified walls were built as extensions of the cliffs, through the Gaspé Peninsula, which we had just left, to the Magdalen Islands, a beach-rung archipelago in the middle of the Gulf, where we were going.

With their sandstone cliffs and flat, shorn plateaus, the Magdalen Islands resemble pies at which someone kept chipping away with a fork but couldn't quite finish. Without any pesky trees in the way (most have been claimed for lumber and firewood), the peculiar topography of the isles lies bare in all directions. In some patches, the turf squishes itself into nubby wrinkles. In others, plateaus remain flat except for the occasional bald hill: bubbles in the piecrust.

Unlike Percé, many of the residents of the Magdalen Islands, or Madelinots, stay on the archipelago year round, which meant we would be foraging beyond the frozen food aisle. However, to pay homage to our bonding with the tourtières, we felt compelled to try its maritime cousin: *pot-en-pot*, a pie filled with seafood—one of the archipelago's traditional offerings we found at a restaurant near our bed and breakfast.

The pie's sweet gravy alone provided all the carbs necessary for playing hide-and-seek in the arched holes of the red rocky cliffs on the beaches of Havre aux Maisons, the centermost island. We were far from the first spelunkers; deep inside the beach-facing caves, I found a few clusters of empty beer bottles. We stopped exploring the caves, inviting as they were, because we acquired the distinct feeling that we might walk in on a couple making little Madelinots under a bunch of blankets. Or perhaps the minds of two freshly engaged people imagine such things.

THE ARCHIPELAGO teems with Internet connections, visits from touring indie rock bands, and fuel-efficient Japanese cars. Yet no matter where we traveled in the sparse archipelago, McMansions remained absent. Some of the clapboard houses, seeming too small to contain more than one room, appeared as if they were built over 200 years ago when the islands served as a refuge for French speakers expelled from the Canadian colonies by the British. Even in the 1800s, when British colonial oppression reached the shores of the islands, the Madelinots still managed to build the happiest-looking homes, despite being forced to pay rent on land they had owned and worked for generations.

Many of those homes still stand and uncannily exemplify the Quebecois slogan *"Je me souviens,"* or "I remember." Along the driveways, pudgy fishing boats propped up on steel drums—accompanied by stacks of lobster traps—provided the standard yard ornaments for the winter, telling of the island's most important industry of past and present.

Clamming claims far simpler tools that haven't changed much over the years. As a person who has enjoyed steaming the critters in wine, I decided I would gain a better understanding of the lives of clams if I gathered them myself, to rediscover the connection between land and food hidden in the plastic-wrapped Western world, to hopefully bond with Melanie in yet another culinary adventure. Were these goals noble enough for us to claw into the sand for hours when it's only ten degrees above freezing? I convinced my fiancée to pull a rubber glove over her engagement ring so we could find out.

With a bucket borrowed from our bed and breakfast and a small gardening rake purchased from a grocery store, we walked onto a beach on the northern end of Cap aux Meules Island, heading towards a lagoon known for its clam population. We followed a well-flattened path onto a dune where a few scattered people were bending over and picking something from the sand. This must be the spot, I thought, even though the scrub-bristled terrain seemed more like a dry bog than a beach. *"Palourdes?"* Clams? I asked a graying woman who turned to me and sent me an apprehensive stare. She didn't respond. Perhaps my accent was off. I asked again.

I heard a nearby, drum-like bonk, something being tossed into a bucket. That wasn't a clam. It was a cranberry. That would explain the bog. "Oh, cranberries!" I announced. The woman nodded, her apprehensive stare still intact. "That's okay, I know where your parents made you," I wanted to say, thinking of the island's cozy caves.

When life gives you cranberries, pick 'em. And we did, until we remembered that the tide was coming in and we had to hurry to reach the flats of the lagoon's edge. As with every other time I had walked onto a beach, I wasn't mindful—at first—that just below my feet, thousands of clams could be making their homes. But once we started to look for holes in the sand—signs of clams underneath—the beach revealed another dimension to its wealth, concealed under its beauty. We began to dig. Some clams squirted at us in protest. The sand was cold, the wind colder, but Melanie figured out how to locate the clams much faster than me. Leave it to a chef to master our dinner's entire journey from beach to table.

The owner of the bed and breakfast, Monica, who stays young by playing hockey with her daughter's team, allowed us to use her kitchen to steam our day's bounty. The clams were as tender as oysters, but I never managed to rid them of all their sand (her kitchen did not come equipped with a mollusk spa), making them difficult to enjoy, which only made me respect the work of professional clammers.

Monica returned from the day's game. "We won!" she said, grinning. As we finished the clams, Monica asked,

"Did you see any seals?" She was referring to seals that live in the lagoon year-round. We did not see any on the sand, but we had managed to encounter them earlier in the day at a butcher shop on Cap aux Meules, where we picked up seal terrine *a l'orange* and seal jerky.

Eyeing our seal snacks on the table, Monica mentioned, "We don't eat the species of seal in the lagoon. They don't taste good." That might be why they are still in the lagoon and not inside sausage casings for $32 per kilogram.

While protesters have been voicing their objection to seal hunts (even though many said protesters wear leather shoes), the people of the Magdalen Islands have been relying on seals for everything from oil to clothing to pie fillings for centuries. Seal hunting is not only sustainable—the Gulf of St. Lawrence seal population hasn't been threatened in over forty years since the introduction of hunting quotas—but also seals don't require pastures as with livestock, and hence do not contribute to deforestation and topsoil loss. Seal herds live in the wild—on the ice and in the water. There's no need to inject them with antibiotics to keep them alive, and they will not be fed ground-up brains of their own species, as is the case on some large-scale commercial livestock farms. Seals eat what nature intended for them to eat: wild fish.

And, for the health-conscious out there, seal meat is higher in protein and lower in fat than beef. I began to feel out of touch for having eaten all those meat pies back in Percé. But at the same time, I knew that by buying seal meat, a product not very popular outside Canada's Maritime Provinces, I was supporting the local economy and a Madelinot tradition.

Could seal meat be the protein of the future? That is unlikely, so long as there are enough people who view seals as adorable enough to protect, while viewing pigs, chickens, and lobsters ugly enough to eat.

Protests aside, it's fun to talk about seals in Quebec, because the French word for seal, *phoque*, sounds just like a linguistically versatile curse word in English. You can just imagine the wealth of jokes and puns shared among bilingual Quebecois.

Getting back to our dinner, I would have never guessed that the spicy phoque we shared on the table would be so tender.

A FRIENDLY, SLOBBERING DOG ushered us up the stairs. In the rolls of a wintering farm, we arrived at the tasting room of Le Barbocheux, one of the island's fruit wineries, and like many other businesses of the archipelago, the store was a front room in the proprietor's home.

I saw where the dog had acquired its endearing personality when Léonce, the winemaker and owner, discussed the merits of his swill. "It gets better with age!" Léonce exclaimed of his blueberry port, matching our samples shot for shot. "Call me in a year, you will see!" He instructed us to pour the port into chocolate cups (free with each bottle) when serving, guaranteeing that the bottles we bought would not last long enough to test his promise.

The port, though fleeting, would mark a sweet end to our last day in the Gulf of Saint Lawrence. Earlier, we had driven up the entire fishhook shape of the archipelago. At the 650-resident Anglophone enclave at the bend of the hook, we ate fish and chips served with the Quebecois snack poutine instead of plain fries, an edible harmony in a province with over two hundred years of simmering linguistic rivalry. We visited the seal museum, where we followed a history of sealing, complete with mention of Brigitte Bardot's outcries and a recipe for seal flipper pie.

But it was the travel from island to island—all connected by sand dunes—that had instilled me with the archipelago's stable throb: the cave-ridden cliffs, sharing their shade of red with seal terrine; the stacks of lobster traps resting until next season; the clapboards receiving a fresh coat of mustard-yellow or royal purple; the omega-3 glow in faces of walkers along the roads; the sultry postcard tease of lighthouses posing in smoldering sunsets.

Like the cliffs, an incorrigible life strength runs through the Gulf that has weathered storms, colonial cruelty, icebound winters, shifting seafood stocks—a strength fueled by passionate dedication. Perhaps it's the fuel of romance itself.

Epilogue and Acknowledgements

The popularity of soccer seems to be one of the few common strands that flows throughout the countries I have visited in the Americas, and I have found that travel writing may share a trait with it. In soccer, there are few opportunities to score without assists, and such is the case with the research, interviews, and on-the-ground access that build the framework for a travel story. I was fortunate to be able to walk through cultural portals opened for me by Tatita Marquez and Edelmar Fernando Siqueira in Uruguay; Karl Stanley in Honduras; Cody Clare in Nicaragua; Ram Prashad, Leon Moore, and Charles Ramson in Guyana; Almudena Gutierrez in Venezuela; Felipe Bernal Cuchil and Lawrence Gottschamer in Guatemala; Philip Rae in Quebec; Ismet Bracic in Queens; and Gustavo Torres, in New York City, who shared his experiences on the Amazonian side of Peru. I'd like to especially thank Major Kerry Najolia and the rest of the Jefferson Parish SWAT team for letting me tag along for an evening's nutria hunt along the canals of New Orleans.

My wife Melanie has been the sparkle in my life and the companion of my travels since long before *The Panama News* editor Eric Jackson, in a 2006 review of my first book, referred to her as the "foxy Filipina-American lady" in my life. Telling of the bond Melanie and I have created while traveling, we decided to get married on Île d'Orléans, Quebec, a few years after we tandem-biked our way around the island. Melanie has shown patience and support for my travel projects, even with my most bizarre and obsessive outings, so she deserves the grandest thanks of them all, and as always, I look forward to hitting the road with her and sharing whatever new experiences and flavors we encounter.

Bibliography

Brazil

"Reseña cronológica de Chuy (1885 - 1888)." *Chuynet*
(http://www.chuynet.com/portal/historial/008-1885-1888).
"Reseña cronológica de Chuy (1964 - 1966)." *Chuynet*
(http://www.chuynet.com/portal/historial/018-1964-1966).

Canada

Lyon, David. "Matters of the Harp." Robb Report, 1 December 2005
(http://robbreport.com/luxury-travel/Journeys-Matters-of-the-
Harp?artcle=12009).
Pfeiff, Margo. "In Quebec, Isles of Splendid Isolation." *Los Angeles Times*, 21
April 2002 (http://www.latimes.com/travel/la-042102quebec-story.html).

Chile

Palmer, Rod. *Street Art Chile*. Corte Madera: Gingko Press, 2008.
Soto, Renzo. *Super Vaca: Historias Negras*. Valparaiso: Libra Impresores, 2008.

Ecuador

Meisch, Lynn. *Andean Entrepreneurs: Otavalo Merchants and Musicians in the
Global Arena*. Austin: University of Texas Press, 2002.
Miller, Tom. *The Panama Hat Trail*. Washington, D.C.: National Geographic
Adventure Press, 2001.

Guatemala

Goetz, Delia and Morley, Sylvanus (translators). *Popul Vuh: The Sacred Book of
the Ancient Quiché Maya By Adrián Recinos*. Norman, Oklahoma: University of
Oklahoma Press, 1950.
Parker, Janet and Stanton, Julie (ed). *Mythology: Myths, Legends and Fantasies*.
Cape Town: Struik Publishers, 2003. p 481.

Guyana

Harris, Jessica B. *Beyond Gumbo: Creole Fusion Food from the Atlantic Rim.* New York: Simon & Schuster, 2003. p 226.

Pharmaceutical Journal and Transactions, Third Series, Volume XVII, 1886-1887. London: J & A Churchill, 1887. p 411.

"Road fatalities reduced in Berbice in 2008." *Kaieteur News Online*, 5 January 2009 (http://www.kaieteurnewsonline.com/2009/01/05/road-fatalities-reduced-in-berbice-in-2008/).

Honduras

"Our History." RoatanMarinePark.com (http://www.roatanmarinepark.com/about/history/).

Nicaragua

Floyd, Troy S. *The Anglo-Spanish Struggle for Mosquitia.* Albuquerque: University of New Mexico Press, 1967.

Rushdie, Salman. *The Jaguar Smile: A Nicaraguan Journey.* New York: Picador, 1997.

Panama

Howe, James. *A People Who Would Not Yield: Panama, the United States, and the San Blas Kuna.* Washington: Smithsonian Institution Press, 1998.

Peru

"Diners lured by super guinea pig." *BBC News*, 23 October 2004 (http://news.bbc.co.uk/2/hi/americas/3946771.stm).

Trinidad & Tobago

Kangalee, Gerry. "Out of pain this culture was born." *Trinbagopan*, 21 August 2008 (http://www.trinbagopan.com/articles/210808b.htm).

Holiday Magazine's Travel Guide to the Caribbean. New York: Random House, 1961. p 128.

United States

Brenner, Joel Glenn. "U Street: A U-Turn to Renewal." *The Washington Post*, 6 November 1993.

Cooper, Christopher: "Louisiana Is Trying To Turn Pest Into a Meal." *The New York Times*, 14 December, 1997.

Vargas, Jose Antonio. "The Changing Complexion of U Street." *The Washington Post*, 16 April 2005.

Uruguay

Montaño, Oscar D. "Candombe, herencia africana en el Uruguay." Candombe.com.uy (http://www.candombe.com.uy/historia_seccion1.html).

Trigona, Marie. "Uruguay: Spirit of Afro Resistance Alive in Candombe."
Upside Down World
(http://upsidedownworld.org/main/content/view/1145/48/).

Venezuela
Wilpert, Gregory. "The Economics, Culture, and Politics of Oil in Venezuela."
Venezuela Analysis (http://venezuelanalysis.com/analysis/74).

About the Author

Darrin DuFord has written food and travel pieces for the *San Francisco Chronicle, World Hum, BBC Travel, Roads & Kingdoms, Perceptive Travel, Transitions Abroad,* and *McSweeney's Internet Tendency,* among others. His debut book *Is There a Hole in the Boat? Tales of Travel in Panama Without a Car* won a silver medal in the 2007 Lowell Thomas Travel Journalism Awards and was chosen by *Foreword Magazine* as a finalist for their 2006 Book of the Year Awards. In 2011, he co-founded Mel's Melting Pot, a small-batch sauce and condiment company, with his wife Melanie. Their products integrate flavors and spices they have encountered during their travels. He lives with his wife and son in Queens, New York, America's most diverse county.

For links to his latest articles, visit his website http://www.OmnivorousTraveler.com. Follow him on Twitter at @darrinduford.

11/16

WITHDRAWN

36778047R00176

Made in the USA
Middletown, DE
11 November 2016